Critical Guides to Spanish Texts

EDITED BY J. E. VAREY AND A. D. DE

Critical Guides to Spanish Texts

10 Sarmiento : Facundo

SARMIENTO

Facundo

C. A. Jones
Fellow of Trinity College, Oxford

Grant & Cutler Ltd *in association with*
Tamesis Books Ltd 1974

© Grant & Cutler Ltd
1974
ISBN 0 900411 76 7
Printed in England at
The Compton Press Ltd
for
GRANT & CUTLER LTD
11 BUCKINGHAM STREET, LONDON, W.C.2

Contents

for Mary

Preface

It is almost impossible to remain neutral about Sarmiento's *Facundo*. On the one hand it has been hailed as not only the first great work of Argentine literature, but as the most original and powerful book written in America up to the time of its publication in 1845;[1] on the other hand it has been dismissed as a badly-written and ephemeral piece of journalism, lacking form and depth alike (cf. *3*, 459).

Facundo is also a baffling book. It takes its title from the name of an obscure *caudillo* or local leader whose power rested upon terrorism and cunning; but the figure of Juan Facundo Quiroga often merges into the type he represents, the *gaucho malo,* or else serves as a means to attack a much more powerful and dangerous enemy, Juan Manuel Rosas, the dictator of the Argentine Republic, whose reign of terror lasted effectively from 1829 to 1852. More disturbing is that the book, which is meant to be an attack on Quiroga and the *gaucho* as the embodiment of the barbarism which Sarmiento sees as the threat to Argentinian progress, shows what looks like a sneaking regard for both Quiroga and the *gaucho,* and that the conflict between *Civilización y barbarie,* the opposing forces of the work's subtitle, is blurred by the obvious admiration for the strength and glamour of the upholders of barbarism. Sarmiento is not of course the first biographer to be won over by a subject that he sets out to attack, but the results are bound to be disconcerting.

Then again, no-one knows where to place the work. Apart from deciding whether it is a history, a sociological study or a work of literature – it has been praised and condemned under

1. "El más original y poderoso de los libros escritos hasta entonces en América, el 'Facundo' . . ." A. Zum Felde, *Indice crítico de la literatura hispanoamericana. El ensayo y la crítica,* Mexico City, 1954, p. 100. It has been seen as the *Don Quixote* of America (cf. Sansón Carrasco, "Sarmiento en la brega", in *El Nacional,* 21 November 1885, quoted by A. W. Bunkley, *6,* 508-9).

all three headings – it refuses to be contained within any clearly definable genre or style.[2]

Page references to *Facundo* are to *Facundo. Civilización y barbarie,* ed. Raimundo Lazo, Mexico City, Editorial Porrúa, 1966. Although printed in double columns, and with a rather generous sprinkling of misprints, this is the most easily accessible edition. For a critical edition, reference should be made to that of Alberto Palcos (Universidad Nacional de la Plata, 1938). *Facundo* is contained in volume 7 of the 52-volume edition of the *Obras de D.F. Sarmiento publicadas bajo los auspicios del Gobierno argentino,* 1899-1909.

The figures in parenthesis in italic type refer to the numbered items in the Select Bibliography; the italic figure is usually followed by a page reference.

I am very grateful to Mrs. Catherine Ross, who typed the final version of this book. My illness at the time of arrival of the page proofs drove me to seek the generous help of my friend and colleague, F. W. Hodcroft, who read and corrected the proof on my behalf.

2. Cf. beginning of Chapter 5.

1. The author

Domingo Faustino Sarmiento is a figure no less fascinating and baffling than the work with which his name is chiefly associated. The son of a romantic but somewhat irresponsible adventurer, José Clemente Sarmiento, and of a woman of strength and immense patience and endurance as well as resource, Paula Albarracín, he was born in the capital of the province of San Juan de la Frontera, at the foot of the Andes, and, as the name suggests, near the border of Chile – about as far away from the capital of Argentina, Buenos Aires, as it was possible to be. This fact is not without its importance in accounting for the attitudes which Sarmiento was later to assume; and the date of his birth, 15 February 1811, followed soon after the establishment of an independent republic in what had previously been a part of the great Spanish colonial empire, the Viceroyalty of La Plata, set up as recently as 1776, although the area, as part of the vast Viceroyalty of Peru, had been under Spanish domination since the first half of the sixtenth century. Both Sarmiento's parents were of pure Spanish blood, descended from long-established families; but this did not prevent him from professing a deep hatred of Spain which lost its bitterness to some extent when he eventually visited the Peninsula in 1846, but which remained one of the keynotes of his thinking and emotional makeup throughout his life. The great Spanish writer and thinker, Miguel de Unamuno, remarked that Sarmiento's antipathy towards Spain showed more clearly than anything how essentially Spanish he was, since he hated those things about the country which Spaniards themselves never ceased to complain about.[3] Sarmiento tells us a good deal about his early life and ex-

---

3. "Porque, en efecto, Sarmiento hablaba mal de España en español, y como los españoles lo hacemos, maldiciendo de nuestra tradición las mismas cosas que de ella maldecimos los españoles y de la misma manera que las maldecimos . . ." Unamuno, "Algunas consideraciones sobre la literatura hispano-americana", in *Ensayos*, VII, Madrid, 1919, p. 105.

periences in a work entitled *Recuerdos de provincia,* which he
published in 1850, five years after the appearance of *Facundo,* and
which many critics, including the pioneer North American His-
panist George Ticknor, have considered to be his masterpiece
from the literary point of view.[4] After a short period of schooling
under the guidance of the Rodríguez brothers, who might be
described as experimental educational missionaries, Sarmiento
found himself as the manager of the local store, which was
owned by his aunt, and which he kept for over a year, during
which he took the opportunity to read widely and voraciously
almost anything which came into his hands, with the main emphasis on works which could be described as revolutionary in aim.
This youthful self-education, in which he did receive some guidance from his uncle José de Oro, a priest, was to serve him very
well in his later political career, just as his rather limited formal
schooling was to leave him with a lifelong interest in educational
theory and methods. His reading, which seems to have been more
or less a process of devouring books for the sake of the ideas
which they contained rather than for their literary appeal, explains the wide-ranging interests which are obvious in his own
works, as well as the essentially experimental attitude which we
never fail to find in them. The Argentine novelist Manuel Gálvez,
in a not altogether favourable biography, remarks that if he were
asked to sum up the characteristics of Sarmiento as a writer, he
would say that he was first and foremost and at all times a journalist, concerned to get hold of and purvey as quickly and effectively
as possible information about any subject under the sun (3, 446-7).
Sarmiento first demonstrated his rebellious nature when, in
1828, he was called up for military service by the Governor of San
Juan province, Manuel Quiroga. He submitted a protest in writing
to the Governor against what he considered to be an intolerable
personal inconvenience, and was summoned to appear in person
before Quiroga, against whom he continued to wage a feud for
some time. It will be necessary to explain in somewhat more detail later the political and military situation in Argentina in the
first decades of the nineteenth century, in order to understand the
growth of Sarmiento as a leading figure in the public life of his

4. Cf. A. Belín Sarmiento, *Sarmiento anecdótico,* Saint Cloud, 1929, p. 46.

country.[5] As between the two main contending parties in the republic, the unitarians and the federalists, Sarmiento sided with the former and against the domination of Buenos Aires province, whose governors by tradition became the leaders of the nation, and who carried out their duties very much in the manner of the local tyrants, relying on force and influence to exercise their oppressive and intolerant rule. As a result of his defiance of Quiroga, and of his political attitudes in general, Sarmiento was imprisoned and threatened with execution, but eventually released and allowed to return home. However, it was obvious that so long as Quiroga remained in power, there would be no peace or security for Sarmiento, and in 1831, in company with his father and other unitarian sympathisers, he took refuge in Chile, where he was to spend a good many years of his life, engaged in journalism and in political activities. It was during this first stay in Chile that Sarmiento became the father of an illegitimate daughter, Faustina, and began the serious study of foreign languages, especially French and English, which he never managed to speak well, but which he learned in order to be able to read and translate works which fed his progressive and liberal yearnings, rather than books which appealed for their aesthetic qualities. At first engaged in commerce, Sarmiento soon went to work in the mines, where he astonished his companions by his assiduous devotion to study even in the pits, and where he contracted a serious illness, which eventually led him to return to Argentina, to the province of San Juan of which he was a native. Here he began to be interested in literature more purely for its own sake, and founded a literary society which showed a leaning towards the works of the French Romantics. Sarmiento made some attempts himself at writing poetry, but they were never very successful, and the unsympathetic criticism of them by the statesman and literary pundit Juan Bautista Alberdi may have been the beginning of a long-standing conflict between the two men, who were temperamentally and ideologically incompatible in almost every way.[6] One can-

5. Cf. below, Chapter 2.
6. On the subject of Sarmiento and poetry cf. *10*, 99-104. On Alberdi's attitude to Sarmiento's poetry cf. *6*, 105-6. For a more general treatment of the differences between Sarmiento and Alberdi cf. A. Zum Felde, *Indice crítico* p. 102, and *5*, 125-7.

not resist the suspicion that Sarmiento, for all the breadth of his interests and his intellectual curiosity, was something of a philistine, yet one who was capable of producing a kind of poetry, more evident perhaps when he was writing impassioned prose than when he was composing verse.

It was a year after his return home from Chile, in 1839, that Sarmiento's lifelong interest in journalism led to the foundation of his first newspaper, *El Zonda*, a short-lived venture which came to an end when, with the triumph of the federals, the party of the dictator Rosas to which Sarmiento was opposed, Sarmiento was once more thrown into prison. The events of that same year, 1840, put an end to another venture of the author of *Facundo*, in a cause which remained very near to his heart throughout the rest of his life. This cause was the education of women, and it was in 1839 that Sarmiento had set up in San Juan a college for young women, Santa Rosa, where he tried to put into action his belief that women, as the future mothers of the nation, not only deserved but needed the training which would fit them for their vital and responsible task of bringing up the citizens who were to make Argentina the great democratic republic of which he dreamed and for which he worked untiringly, if only partially successfully.[7] It would not be accurate to think of Sarmiento as a forerunner of women's liberation, however, and the programme of studies which he laid down is one which seems frighteningly rigorous to modern eyes, involving an almost unceasing devotion to books and discussion, which must have made the inmates of his college much more like secular nuns than modern emancipated young ladies. Sarmiento, always amorously inclined, had the misfortune to fall in love with one of his pupils, whose parents, almost certainly with good reason, did not consider his situation or his character sufficiently stable to make him a satisfactory match.

Imprisoned by the federals in 1840, and with the threat of execution once more hanging over him, Sarmiento managed to escape and, for the second time in his young life, took refuge again in Chile, hurling defiance as he went at the forces of Rosas

7. For an account of Sarmiento's educational reform, cf. E. Correas, *Sarmiento and the United States,* Gainesville, University of Florida Press, 1961, pp. 3-4, 8, 10, 12, 13, 25, 29, 31 and 39.

,which had destroyed the projects that he had set under way, and which had come so near to destroying him too. This time his mother and the rest of his family went with him, and he settled down, as far as his restless nature would allow, to a career as a journalist, supporting the conservative cause and becoming a friend of the Minister Manuel Montt, whose encouragement was almost certainly the major factor in bringing about the writing of *Facundo* in 1845. The novelist Gálvez, whose life of Sarmiento has been mentioned before, attributes this political about-turn to the opportunism which he regards as typical of the journalist's makeup;[8] but before one assumes too much, one must be aware not only of the nature of conservatism in the Chile of the period, but also of Sarmiento's attitudes in other spheres of activity, which show him as still very much the liberal reformer. The government of Manuel Bulnes, which lasted from 1841 to 1851, although avowedly conservative, was sympathetic towards liberals in Chile, and was in itself to a large extent progressive. Manuel Montt, as a member of the government, was devoted, like Sarmiento, to the cause of educational reform, and it was in 1842 that the University of Chile was founded, with Andrés Bello, the Venezuelan poet and grammarian, as its first rector. Oddly enough, Sarmiento did not get on with Bello as well as one might have expected, and this in spite of the fact that Bello supported the Argentinian in one of his wilder schemes, that which aimed at the radical reform of orthography.[9] The truth is that Bello, for all his advanced liberal ideas in some spheres, was a purist in linguistic matters, and Sarmiento was anything but orthodox in his views on linguistic usage and literary excellence, and refused to make obeisance to the great saints in the literary calendar, including even figures like the Italianate sixteenth-century Tole-

8. "Fue la encarnación de la inestabilidad. Jamás un hombre se ha contradecido tanto. El contradecirse es propio del periodista" (p. 448).
9. Those who consult works of Sarmiento published under his direction before 1852 will note the peculiarities of his orthography. This was a subject on which he held strong views, which he felt obliged to modify later in his life. Apart from such differences, which are apparent in the bibliographical reference (see below note 15), Sarmiento's reforms do not amount to anything very fundamental. Fernando de Herrera and Juan Ramón Jiménez are two Spanish poets who dabbled with the same kind of reforms; Bernard Shaw wanted to do something similar, perhaps with better reason, for English.

dan poet Garcilaso de la Vega and the learned Augustinian humanist from Salamanca, Fray Luis de León.[10]

Sarmiento was given a chair in the Faculty of Philosophy and Humanities in the newly founded University of Chile in the year after its foundation, 1843; but he was not destined to be a "remote and ineffectual don", and he continued his fight against Rosas and the federalists throughout his stay in Chile, where his enemies pursued him to Santiago with an order for extradition delivered by Rosas's special ambassador, Baldomero García, which the government of Chile refused to accept. Sarmiento had written *Mi defensa*, which was published in 1843, but in the face of repeated attacks, Montt encouraged him to write another book in answer to his enemies.[11] As a result of following this suggestion, *Facundo* was written in the short period of two months during May and June of 1845, being published in instalments first of all in the newspaper *El Progreso* and later as a supplement to the same journal. It came out at the end of July in book form under the title *Civilización y barbarie. Vida de Juan Facundo Quiroga*, and was then circulated in pamphlet form again in *El Nacional* of Montevideo, from October of the same year.[12]

Acting as the agent of Montt, Sarmiento was sent off on an extensive tour of Europe, Africa and North America, to study educational methods. While its author was in France, *Facundo* came to the notice of the *Revue des Deux Mondes* and began to attract the attention which it had largely failed to do in South America, but which it has never ceased to do since, throughout the Spanish-speaking world and indeed beyond. In North America Sarmiento sought out the Massachusetts educational theorist and reformer, Horace Mann, with whom he formed a firm bond of friendship and mutual admiration. It was Mann's wife Mary, who was to become a lifelong friend and confidante,

10. Cf. below (p. 35).
11. "Contésteles con un libro." Cf. *5*, 292-3.
12. For the early history of *Facundo* editions, cf. G. Ara, "Las ediciones del *Facundo*", in *Revista Iberoamericana*, XXIII, July-December 1958, no. 46, pp. 375-94; E. Carilla, "Dos ediciones del *Facundo*", in *Boletín de literaturas hispánicas*, Santa Fe, Universidad Nacional del Litoral, no. 1, 1959 (on the Spanish and English editions of 1868); and Verdevoye, *1*, 500 and *passim*.

who translated *Facundo* into English,[13] and who did a great deal towards improving Sarmiento's spoken English, which by all accounts was never very impressive, in spite of her efforts. Before returning to Argentina in 1849, Sarmiento had married Benita Martínez Pastoriza, a lady of his native San Juan by whom he had already had a son whose original name had been Domingo Fidel Castro, but who adopted the name of Sarmiento after his father's marriage, and to whom he remained deeply devoted throughout the rest of his life. His marriage with Benita did not survive the strains of his restless temperament and wandering existence, and he became estranged from her in 1862; but his sentimental attachment to their child was one of the lasting satisfactions that he found for the warm and sentimental side of his nature which shows through in any detailed account of his life and works, and which is a hallmark of his writings.

On his return to Argentina, Sarmiento had published a work entitled *Viajes en Europa, Africa y América*;[14] and it was to be followed a year later, in 1850, by another work of a very different nature, and one in which his idealism ran away with him more than anywhere else in his writing. This was *Argirópolis*, one of whose most far-fetched ideas was the setting up of a new capital for a federal system to include the States of Argentina, Uruguay and Paraguay, on the remote island of Martín García from which a thoroughly democratic federation of states would be equitably and progressively governed.[15] This book gained very little support, and was harshly attacked by Alberdi, who had already condemned Sarmiento's *Facundo* as a work not only badly written and constructed but based on false premisses about the nature of the state of Argentina (*14*). It was in the same year as *Argirópolis* that Sarmiento published *Recuerdos de provincia*, a personal and nostalgic work which, lacking the controversial elements of the

---

13. The title of Mrs. Horace Mann's English translation, which is followed by a biography of Sarmiento, is *Life in the Argentine Republic in the Days of the Tyrants; or, Civilization and Barbarism*, etc., New York, Hurd and Houghton, 1868.

14. Santiago de Chile, Julio Belín i Cia, 1849.

15. The full title was *Arjirópolis o la capital de los Estados confederados Del Río de la Plata*, Santiago de Chile, J. Belín i Cia.

two works just mentioned, earned him almost unqualified praise from critics.

The long reign of terror associated with the name of Juan Manuel Rosas met with a challenge in 1851 from Justo José de Urquiza, previously one of Rosas's supporters and the governor of Entre Ríos province, just north of Buenos Aires. Sarmiento lent his support to Urquiza, who gave him a position in his army, and who was eventually successful in overpowering Rosas. Sarmiento was not satisfied for long with the new ruler, whom he accused of adopting the same tactics as the old dictator. As far as one can understand, Urquiza was in fact a moderate and relatively progressive leader, surprisingly so for one who was still very much in the *caudillo* tradition; but it was perhaps this latter fact rather than his actual policy or conduct which alienated the sympathy of Sarmiento, who was always an idealist, perhaps too much so for his own good.[16] At any rate, Sarmiento returned once more to Chile where, with the exception of one short visit in 1854, he was to remain for three years. When he did return finally to Argentina, he went to live in Buenos Aires province, returning to the pampa, which he had first seen in 1851, in Urquiza's campaign against Rosas, but which he had described so vividly in *Facundo* as long ago as 1845.[17] He was delighted to find that the picture he had drawn from his imagination and from

16. For a brief account of Urquiza's presidency cf. *7*, 329-32.
17. Cf. Belín Sarmiento, *Sarmiento anecdótico* pp. 67-8. A. Palcos comments: "Valido de su maravilloso poder intuitivo y de su rica imaginación, le bastan para evocarla [the pampa], la lectura de viajeros como Azara, Head y Andrews, los cantos de Echeverría y las gráficas descripciones que oye en boca de los arrieros sanjuaninos y de los militares argentinos residentes en Chile . . ." (*10*, 36). Sarmiento's sensitivity to natural beauty is a constant feature of his work. It anticipates a fundamental characteristic of Latin-American writing, and has an important function as background to character in the work of Sarmiento. A. M. Barrenechea, in "Función estética y significación histórica de las campañas pastoras en el *Facundo*", in *Nueva revista de filología hispánica*, Mexico, XV, nos. 1-2, 1961, pp. 309-24, writes: "La naturaleza americana tiene a menudo, en Sarmiento, la función de resonador de un personaje o una acción, que así adquiere notas de misterio, de intensidad salvaje, de grandeza áspera o solemne" (p. 316). On the accuracy of Sarmiento's picture of the pampa, Palcos, *10*, p. 37, quotes Pedro de Angelis, normally hostile to Sarmiento, as saying: "Esto se mueve, es la Pampa; el pasto hace ondas agitadas por el aire, se siente el olor de las yerbas amargas".

his reading had been remarkably accurate: incidentally, among
the many criticisms which were levelled against *Facundo* no one
ever, so far as I know, accused Sarmiento of being inaccurate in
his description of the countryside, which formed so important a
part in showing up the background of "the Tiger of the Plains",
as Facundo Quiroga was known.

Urquiza's rule lasted until 1862, and during the latter part of
his period of government Sarmiento made his living as a journalist, as well as engaging in politics. Urquiza was succeeded by a
unitarian, General Bartolomé Mitre, whom many consider to
have been the greatest Argentinian after San Martín, the liberator
of the country from Spanish rule at the beginning of the nineteenth century. Although a soldier, and one who gained the rule
over his country by military force, Mitre put an end to the era of
caudillism.[18] Sarmiento found himself the elected governor of his
native province of San Juan, and in this position was at last free
to put into operation some of his plans for reform. Not unex-
pectedly, he did so against powerful opposition from conservative
forces, and many of his far-reaching plans were thwarted. After
three years in office, he was glad of the opportunity to escape
which came as a result of his appointment by Mitre as minister
plenipotentiary of the Argentine Republic in the United States.
One gets the impression from reading about Sarmiento's life that
he was in a strange way accident-prone; and one is somehow not
surprised to learn that he lost his credentials on the way to Wash-
ington and was forced to wait about for some months before they
arrived and he could present them to the new president, Johnson,
who had succeeded Lincoln, assassinated in the Civil War. At
all events, Sarmiento seems to have used his time profitably while
in North America, and was showered with honours, including an

18. This is a controversial point. Alberdi, who considered Sarmiento as just one
more *caudillo*, would certainly not have agreed. Chapman writes: "The
year 1862, when Mitre ascended to power, is often regarded as the turning-
point in Argentinian history, marking the end of the age of caudillism and
the beginning of national feeling. Only by hindsight can this be called
true, for it would seem that most of the issues were postponed for settlement
until 1880" (7, 332). Earlier in the same work (7, 110), Chapman had written: "Finally, over *all* of Hispanic America there is still the possibility of a
return to caudillism." Recent events in Argentina will bear out the accuracy
of this assessment.

honorary doctorate from the University of Michigan. He always showed a great admiration for the United States, whose stability and progress he attributed to its English heritage. Among the North Americans for whom he showed unqualified admiration was Benjamin Franklin; and he also formed associations with American writers, including Emerson and Longfellow.

Sarmiento returned to his country to find that he had become President, the first elected and the first civilian president Argentina had known. The news of this election reached him as the *Merrimac*, the ship in which he was travelling from the United States, stopped in Rio de Janeiro, and he took over office from Mitre on 12 October, Columbus Day, of 1868. His presidency achieved an enormous amount, although it is by no means clear that it achieved anything like as much as Sarmiento had hoped, and the failures which were interspersed among the successes seem to have left him sad and disillusioned at the end of his period of office.[19] The truth is that, whereas most politicians, in the face of the realities of office, sacrifice their ideals at least to some extent, the degree to which Sarmiento seems to have done so was, so far as one can ascertain, minimal; and he was unable to find comfort for his disillusionment in compromise.[20]

Sarmiento never lost interest in or concern for the causes to which he had been devoted throughout his life. Among these causes that of education, whose status had always been very low

19. Ricardo Rojas, in *El profeta de la pampa. Vida de Sarmiento,* Buenos Aires, 1945, writes: "La situación del país en los seis años terribles, así en la política exterior como en la interna — sexenio de desorden, de sangre y de miseria —, habría quebrado a cualquier otro que no poseyera el temple de Sarmiento" (p. 517). For an account of Sarmiento's trials and achievements as president, cf. *6*, 467-73 and 483. Sarmiento was the victim of at least one attempt at assassination, in 1873 (cf. *6*, 459).

20. Again, not all would agree, and many students of Sarmiento's career have pointed to his arbitrary and authoritarian attitudes and actions during his presidency. Even Bunkley, a sympathetic biographer, writes: "Sarmiento himself, in spite of all his good intentions, was representative of this new caudillism . . . There are three elements of Sarmiento's governmental method that are open to question in this respect. The first of these was his conception of the strong position of the executive branch. The second was his use of interventions to overcome opposition in the interior. And the last was his use of the 'state of siege' and his suspension of guarantees in order to suppress sedition or rebellion" (*6*, 472-3).

in the South American countries, was probably the one nearest of all to his heart; and after his six-year term of office had expired in 1874, as well as occupying the elected post of senator, representing his native province of San Juan, he did not think it beneath his dignity to fill the office of superintendent of schools in Buenos Aires.[21]

Even as a young man, Sarmiento had been taken for one ten or twenty years older than he was; and as early as his second period in the United States, from 1865 to 1868, he was giving the impression of an ageing man, despite the restless vigour with which he entered into every enterprise that came his way. His last years showed little sign that he had lost his mental vigour or agility, but he was tired and ill, and eventually went into retirement in Paraguay, where he died on 11 September 1888, at the age of seventy-seven.

21. Sarmiento's interest and achievements in the sphere of education are attested on several occasions by Bunkley (6, 377, 468 and 488). On p. 468 he writes: "Sarmiento's efforts in the educational field had a lasting effect. Today almost every child of school age in Argentina attends some institution of learning or another. Argentina can boast the best primary educational system in South America and one of the best in the world." As evidence of the low esteem in which education was generally held in South America before Sarmiento's day, Bunkley had earlier quoted the newspaper *El Araucano*, which carried a report of a young Argentinian exile in Chile, who was caught stealing the silver candlesticks from a church, and whose sentence consisted of a term of three years teaching in a small country school. Paul Verdevoye naturally devotes much attention to this aspect (*1*).

2. The historical background

In writing about a figure who for much of his life was in the fore-
front of events in his country, it is perhaps not entirely appro-
priate to separate him from that country's circumstances, and to
talk of a historical background. Much of that background will in
any case have been hinted at in sketching the story of Sarmiento's
life and works. Nevertheless, the study of *Facundo* requires some
knowledge of the course of Argentine history in the nineteenth
century. The movement towards Argentine independence began
in 1810. The impulse towards independence was the result both
of the growing desire for liberation from the colonial power on
the part of white creoles, born and bred in the South American
countries, and of the breakdown in Spain itself of the institution
of monarchy and the old authority which depended upon it. It is
not really our concern to trace the independence movement in
detail here; but the important fact to remember is that it in effect
substituted one form of white aristocratic domination for another,
and left out of account the classes and races which made up the
majority of the country's population. The first revolution was
soon succeeded by another in which the country revolted against
the cities[22] or, as Sarmiento was to put it, the forces of barbarism
revolted against civilisation. In Argentina, as in so many other
Latin-American countries, the era of independence soon gave way
to what has been called the age of the *caudillos*. One of the best
accounts of this period is given by C. E. Chapman (7). "Broadly
defined", says Chapman, "the caudillos were military men, almost literally on horseback, who were at the same time political
bosses and absolute rulers, either of a country or of a district, not-
withstanding the alleged existence of republics and democracies,
and despite the contrary provisions of constitutions and laws"

22. Bartolomé Mitre is quoted (7, 53) as having written: "The true revolution,
the revolution which stirs society, which tends to dominate it and fixes its
destinies for the future, is continued among the very revolutionary peoples
themselves, tearing one another to bits." This has a curiously modern ring.

(p. 106). The *caudillos* were already in existence during the wars of independence, and were to be found fighting both for and against the forces of independence, as the cases of Boves and Páez in Venezuela show. They sprang up as representatives of popular and local interests, which were not upheld by the new leaders of the independence movements, any more than they had been, in practice at least, by the Spanish colonial authority. Throughout the changeover from colonies to republics, as Chapman goes on to point out, "The only real 'patriotism' was, not for Spain or Portugal – not even for a Mexico, Chile, or Brazil – but for one's own city or village" (p. 111). The *conquistadores,* even the colonial viceroys, were very like *caudillos* in the way they carried out their offices, and the wars only encouraged the already built-in tendencies to rally to leaders whose influence and power grew until they could wield the authority of a Facundo Quiroga, or even a Rosas, or a Perón.

Many of the leaders, or *caudillos*, were *gauchos*, the Argentinian equivalents of cowboys. There are, in fact, a number of technical differences between the *gaucho* and the cowboy, but one of the essential differences is that the *gaucho* tended to be an outlaw from society, or at least an outsider, in a way the cowboy never was. All the delinquent tendencies which went with the type were merely encouraged by the access of power and the opportunity to extend the ruthless methods by which they had gained their influence. There are many instances in *Facundo* of the excesses of conduct of which the *gaucho caudillo*, exemplified by Facundo Quiroga, could be capable.

Since the *caudillos* tended to represent local interests, they were opposed to any kind of centralised government, and the coming of independence, bringing as it did a growth in the influence of the *caudillos*, led to a fragmentation of the old colonial authority, which depended upon urban administration. The *caudillos*, almost without exception, it seems safe to say, favoured the system which they called federalism, although, as Kirkpatrick has said, the word was used "in a sense almost opposite to its usual meaning, and implying an effort not at union but at separation".[23] The

23. F. A. Kirkpatrick, *Latin America: a Brief History*, Cambridge University Press, 1938, p. 109.

system involved a great deal of domination by the province of Buenos Aires and its capital city, and the governor of that province, as in the case of Rosas, tended to be dictator of the whole country.

Against the so-called federalists were ranged the unitarians, who, in spite of their name, wanted a genuine democratic federation of provinces, with a properly elected president who would govern in the interests of the whole country. Sarmiento was a life-long unitarian, and it is this conviction which perhaps more than anything accounts for his opposition to such moderate figures as Urquiza, who despite the strong-arm methods whereby he gained control of the country and the exercise of personal power by which he maintained it, was perhaps as progressive in his policies and actions as it was possible at that juncture to be. Sarmiento's own experiences as governor of San Juan and later as president showed that free democratic republicanism was an elusive myth, and he himself has been accused by his critics of being a *caudillo*, the victim of an ethos and a way of life which has perhaps never been thoroughly eradicated in the Argentine. Writing in 1937, Chapman could say, "Over all the countries of Hispanic America, there is still the shadow of the man on horseback" (7, 110). This is still to a large extent true today.

There were, of course, good and bad *caudillos*, just as there have been good and bad kings, and good and bad presidents of republics, even good and bad Prime Ministers. There is considerable agreement, however, that *caudillos* in themselves were a bad thing, and it is difficult to think of anything to say about them that is good. Chapman does find this to say : "The one real service the violent caudillos rendered lay in curbing the turbulence and anarchy of the times. In that, they served the conservatives and masses alike" (p. 116). Oddly enough, it was the *caudillos* who remained in power longest who seem to have been least harmful, for they did manage to achieve some sort of stability, and avoid the violent pendulum of political life which prevailed for most of the time, giving rise to that unending series of revolutions for which Latin America has always been notorious since the end of the colonial power in the southern half of the continent.

From this point of view, Juan Manuel Rosas can be seen as one

of the best of the *gaucho caudillos,* although it is quite certain that
for Sarmiento he was by far the worst, a figure little short of
diabolical. And Sarmiento's view coincides with that of most
Argentinians. Rosas was not a *gaucho* himself, but the son of a
wealthy landowner, and himself a man with considerable commercial interests in the salt-meat business. He used *gauchos* to
establish himself in power, first as governor of Buenos Aires in
1829, and later as ruler of practically the whole of Argentina;
and this association led to his being identified with the *gaucho,*
an identification which owes not a little to Sarmiento's *Facundo.*
He had a band of assassins, known as the *Mazorca,* and his
methods included almost every one associated later with the
Gestapo and the Mafia, while he himself has been described as the
"Machiavelli of the pampas" (7, 328). He was a double-dealer
who did not hesitate to get rid of enemies even when they had
been his closest supporters. One of these figures was Facundo
Quiroga, the subject of Sarmiento's book, who was assassinated
by rivals who were then put to death in turn by Rosas as punishment for their deed. He reduced the *gauchos* from an independent
and tough class of herdsmen and soldiers to a rather pathetic
collection of outlaws and serfs. In so doing he was of course
weakening one of the main threats to the development of peaceful democratic institutions in the Argentine Republic, although
Sarmiento's accusations included one that he was retarding the
progress of his country towards the legitimate republican heritage
which it had earned for itself by throwing off the Spanish yoke.[24]

Rosas's fall, although it seemed unlikely in view of his immense
power and influence, can be seen in the light of subsequent events
to have been inevitable, as in the case of all forms of tyranny.
Rosas maintained his position by suppressing opposition, which
gradually rallied until it became powerful enough to overthrow
him through the efforts of a man who had previously been one of
his chief supporters, Urquiza, who openly opposed him from
1846 until Rosas was finally overpowered in 1852 and went into
exile to live as a farmer near Southampton until his death in
1877.

Sarmiento's biography so far is closely linked with him as the

24. Cf. *Facundo,* pp. 34, 42, 113 and *passim.*

writer of *Facundo*. From now on the author becomes more per-
sonally and directly involved in the historical and political events.
He welcomed Urquiza at first, but soon became disillusioned, as
a result of what one cannot help thinking was a rather short-
sighted attitude (6, 342-5, 351 and 353-4). Urquiza went so far in
the direction of democracy as to call a congress to draw up a
constitution for the Argentine Republic, and adopted peaceful
attitudes in the face of opposition from Buenos Aires, which
feared a loss of power and of its vested interests and held out in
a position of independence for years, while a constitution model-
led on that of the United States was in fact promulgated, one
which gave more power to the central federal government than
in the model. Buenos Aires did not finally join the new setup
until 1859, after Urquiza had defeated an army sent from the
province against the federal government. When Urquiza retired
in 1860, he had achieved something like a modern democratic
state, and he returned to his old job as governor of Entre Ríos
province. He was brought back from his semi-retirement to
defend the federal government, which came under fire from
Buenos Aires as a result of the weakness of Urquiza's successor
as President, Santiago Derqui. Urquiza was defeated by Mitre,
who led the Buenos Aires forces, and who himself became president in 1862. Contrary to what might have been expected, Mitre
did not attempt to put the clock back in favour of Buenos Aires,
except in so far as he succeeded in making Buenos Aires City the
federal capital, but without separating it from the province, which
was not given any special privileges.

This was the state of affairs which Sarmiento inherited when
he assumed the presidency in 1868; and although there were to be
lapses back towards caudillism, it represented a very considerable
advance from the situation which formed the background to
Facundo. It would be going too far to suggest that *Facundo* had
any influence in bringing about the change; but the ideas in it,
pressed by the man who wrote it, were formative and powerful
and, even though some of them were open to question and were
in fact questioned by writers like Alberdi, they underlie the constitutional pattern established by Urquiza and the changes which
were subsequently grafted on to it by Mitre.

3. "Facundo": its aims and achievements

In hinting at the influence which Sarmiento's ideas in *Facundo* may have had in the subsequent development of the Argentine Republic, one must not forget that the book began with a much more negative purpose. It will be remembered that when Sarmiento took refuge in Chile for the second time, he was pursued by the agents of Rosas with an order for his extradition. Sarmiento's deep-seated hatred for the dictator and his agents, which had both personal and political motives, reached boiling point; and it was the Chilean Minister Montt who gave him the advice "Answer them with a book". The book was *Facundo,* written at white heat and published first of all in serial form in *El Progreso,* a Chilean newspaper. It is perhaps important to remember that this work, held up as the first great landmark of Argentine literature and perhaps one of the greatest books produced in Latin America at any time, started off as an extended political pamphlet. What is somewhat mystifying, if one remembers this, is the relatively cool and balanced tone of the work; and also the fact that it is aimed not in fact at Rosas, the arch-enemy, or at least not obviously so. Its target is the much less menacing local *gaucho caudillo,* Facundo Quiroga, who had already been assassinated ten years before, on 18 February 1835. Sarmiento had reason to hate Quiroga, of course, for it was thanks to his arrival in San Juan that Sarmiento had been forced to flee to Chile and lose the chance of higher education on which he had pinned so much hope. Yet one is left with the question why a book which really set out to attack Rosas should ostensibly attack a much less significant figure, who might have remained almost totally unknown were it not for the attention paid to him by his biographer. One answer is that Sarmiento, recognising himself to be a still inexperienced writer, thought it prudent to deal with a subject more easily manageable than the leading

political figure of the country.[25] One might suggest that another
was that Quiroga was a *gaucho,* whereas Rosas, for all his
association with *gauchos,* was not. And Sarmiento associated
with the *gaucho* all the evils which he summed up under the
name of *barbarie,* that barbarism which had held back his
country from the development towards modern democracy that
he had hoped for when the Spanish domination came to an end.
A quotation from the introduction to the book sums up as well
as anything Sarmiento's motives for choosing Facundo as the
focal point of the book :

> Facundo Quiroga . . . es el tipo más ingenuo del carácter de
> la guerra civil de la República Argentina, es la figura más
> americana que la Revolución presenta. Facundo Quiroga
> enlaza y eslabona todos los elementos de desorden que hasta
> antes de su aparición estaban agitándose aisladamente en
> cada provincia; él hace de la guerra local la guerra nacional
> argentina, y presenta triunfante, al fin de diez años de
> trabajos, de devastación y de combates, el resultado de que
> sólo supo aprovecharse el que lo asesinó. He creído explicar
> la revolución argentina con la biografía de Juan Facundo
> Quiroga, porque creo que él explica suficientemente una
> de las tendencias, una de las dos fases diversas que luchan
> en el seno de aquella sociedad singular. (p. 5b)

Facundo Quiroga, then, is a representative figure, more
important for what he stood for than for what he was, or at
least what he was as an individual. For it was important to know
what he was as a type, the type of the *gaucho malo.*

Even when we have reached this point, Sarmiento's motives
in writing the book are not entirely clear, at least when we come
to look at the book itself. For Quiroga, the hated enemy of the

25. A. W. Bunkley writes: "Don Domingo might have chosen any number of
    more important figures than Facundo as a means of telling the history of his
    country, of examining its problems, or of attacking the government of Rosas.
    But he chose Facundo with premeditation and foresight . . . Facundo had
    invaded Sarmiento's own province of San Juan. Don Domingo had had
    personal contact with the caudillo, and many of his friends had had personal
    experiences with him. His less important life would be easier to handle
    for the inexperienced writer, and the implied attack upon Rosas through
    Facundo might be more effective than a direct assault" (6, 207).

author, the representative of barbarism, the *gaucho malo,* emerges as a not unattractive character. As I said earlier, Sarmiento is by no means the first writer to be won over by the subject whom he sets out to attack in his book; and in his own experience, Sarmiento had found it hard to hang on to a loved prejudice after he had visited Spain, just as his visit to France had had the opposite effect of driving away his admiration for that centre of political and cultural progress.

One of Sarmiento's most useful biographers, Alberto Palcos, has suggested that *Facundo* is "the biography that conquered the biographer",[26] and sees Sarmiento's interest in the *gaucho* leader as a reflection of the phenomenon known as titanism, which formed a theme of European Romantic literature in the first half of the nineteenth century.[27] According to this view, Facundo Quiroga stands for the figure who is larger than life, a monster in all senses of the word, but therefore admirable as well as dreadful — indeed perhaps admirable because dreadful. It seems a little unnecessary to pin this down to Romanticism — although there are many aspects of Sarmiento that make one think of him as a Romantic[28] — when one looks for instance at the figure of Satan as presented by Milton, who obviously was not a Romantic, but who drew the figure of the devil in a way which leaves little doubt that he admired him at the same time as he deplored his existence as the enemy of God and the embodiment of all evil.

Another reason why Quiroga fails to come over as the complete villain which he ought really to be stems from his identification with the *gaucho* type, and indeed with one of the worst of the type, the *gaucho malo.* As far as Sarmiento's deliberate purpose is concerned, the *gaucho* calls for outright condemnation as the

26. "Una biografía que conquista al biógrafo" is the sub-heading of one section of 5.
27. Cf. V. Černy, *Essai sur le titanisme dans la poésie romantique occidentale entre 1815 et 1850,* Prague 1935.
28. Américo Castro, writing "En torno al 'Facundo' de Sarmiento", in *Sur,* VIII, August 1938, pp. 26-34, describes *Facundo* as 'un libro de historia, 'more romántico' ". In view of Sarmiento's own opinions about Romanticism — "Writing for the sake of writing" (cf. *6,* 197, quoting an article by Sarmiento in *El Mercurio,* July 29, 1842) — one wonders what he would have made of this.

figure which most menaces the progress of Argentina. Yet it is
quite clear, in the kind of anatomy of the *gaucho* which
Sarmiento presents in the first part of *Facundo,* that he is
fascinated by the *gaucho,* and that he admires many of his gifts,
which are exceptional and indeed uncanny.[29] There is in fact
reason for accusing Sarmiento of exaggeration in his presentation
of the marvellous achievements of the *gaucho rastreador*, the
tracker, for instance. Facundo Quiroga exemplified some of these
uncanny gifts which the *gaucho* possesses, and Sarmiento cannot
help showing his amazement and admiration for his command
over men and situations, even while he hates and disapproves of
so much that the leader stands for.

What the leader stands for is, according to Sarmiento's inter-
pretation, barbarism, the opponent of civilisation. Yet the
author's attitude to barbarism is also equivocal, for at the same
time that it is the enemy of progress, it is strong and vigorous
and uninhibited – and therefore somehow disconcertingly admirable. This is perhaps why Sarmiento found Paris, the centre of
civilisation, so little to his liking, while at the same time he
found himself drawn towards Spain, of which he had been
brought up and educated to disapprove.[30]

So, then, Sarmiento aimed to attack Facundo Quiroga, and
through him the *gaucho caudillo* and the whole barbaric outlook
and way of life for which he stood. We have seen that he
achieved only partial success in carrying out these aims.

But these aims are still to a large extent the negative ones
which Sarmiento had in writing his work. His more positive
aims were to understand the nature of his country and the

29. Paul Verdevoye writes : "Oubliant que les hommes qu'il dépeint sont les
représentants d'une barbarie qu'il déteste, Sarmiento les observe avec autant
de bonne foi que les voyageurs étrangers qui les ont décrits. Au début du
chapitre consacré à la société et à la *pulpería*, il vante, sans un mot de blâme,
le courage du gaucho qui manie le couteau, et l'adresse du cavalier qui saute
dans le fleuve, avec sa monture, pour échapper à la police. Quand il se res-
saisit, pour dire que les grandes qualités humaines, dans une société tyrannisée,
deviennent criminelles, il a déjà brossé des tableaux pleins de vie qui susci-
tent la sympathie plutôt que la réprobation" (*1*, 113-4).
30. A. M. Barrenechea notes how before he wrote *Facundo* Sarmiento had always attributed Argentina's ills to Spain's influence (*13*). Bunkley recalls how
Sarmiento used to refer to the Spaniards as "Goths" (*6*, 70).

personalities of those who had come to rule it.[31] Here the author
seems to have been more successful, although there have been
those, like Alberdi, who maintain that Sarmiento in fact totally
misunderstood the nature of the situation. We shall deal with his
criticism, which is a fundamental one, in a moment.

Although Sarmiento sees the history of his country largely
in terms of its rulers, the rulers are also viewed as essentially
the products of the country which has reared them. This is why,
as he explains in the introduction to *Facundo,* Simón Bolívar, the
great Liberator of Venezuela and the countries of the north, has
been so incompletely understood. He has always been seen by
biographers and historians as if he were a European leader,
whereas the really important thing about him is his American-
ism. It is even more ridiculous to look at Facundo, born and bred
on the Argentine *pampa,* from a European point of view; and yet
artists from Buenos Aires who have represented Facundo have
shown him wearing a frock coat instead of the *gaucho* clothes in
which he invariably appeared.

Sarmiento sets out, then, to show the nature of the Argentine
countryside, and begins with a chapter entitled "Aspecto físico
de la República Argentina, y caracteres, hábitos e ideas que
engendra", going on from there to outline the outstanding
human types to be found in this countryside, and especially the
various tyes of the *gaucho,* sketched in his natural habitat, the
pulpería, a combination of general store and tavern. The first
part of the three of which the book is composed ends with an
account of the revolution of 1810, in which the revolt of the
creoles against the Spaniards was followed almost simultaneously
by the revolt of the *caudillos* against the city; in Sarmiento's own

31. Castro writes: "Pero en Sarmiento la saña contra Quiroga y Rozas [*sic*] es
menos viva que el afán de entenderlos, de hacerlos trascender de la fría soledad de sus conciencias, agotadas en el instante existencial, sordas al rumor de
la misma vida que les otorgaba aquel existir.

"Sarmiento, con ímpetu magnánimo, se arroja a la tarea de explicar [=
desplegar] la vida de Facundo, que a primera vista es una mezcla infeliz de
negaciones amasadas con sangre; concibe entonces la empresa de este libro en
torno al vivir de un hombre, impuesto a su ambiente como una fatal
evidencia, como símbolo de lo que por necesidad natural era a la sazón un
aspecto de la informe y naciente República Argentina . . ." (*11,* 28-9).

words, "Las ciudades triunfan de los españoles, y las campañas
de las ciudades". For Sarmiento this is a disaster, for it is in
Buenos Aires that the centre of European civilisation is to be
found, and in its triumph over the barbarism represented by
Quiroga and the even more formidable Rosas lies the hope for
the future of the Argentine Republic, a hope in which Sarmiento
piously believes.

Although Sarmiento has not really been concerned to take up
the point about Buenos Aires as the centre of civilisation, he has,
I think, successfully shown that Facundo Quiroga, the representative of barbarism, is the product of his environment in the
pampas and of his *gaucho* traditions. He has done here, with a
large measure of success, what he set out to do, and if he is to be
criticised, it seems more fair to direct the criticism to the
premisses from which he worked, and to the factors which he
omitted from consideration. *Facundo* also shows, in its third part,
how Rosas came into and maintained his power for so long, and
makes certain predictions about the future of Argentina, predictions which were largely fulfilled, at least for a time, by
subsequent events.

One fundamental criticism of Sarmiento's thesis, which sets
out from the belief that the identification of civilisation with
Buenos Aires and barbarism with the *pampa* is excessively close,
is that expressed by Juan Bautista Alberdi in his book *La barbarie
histórica de Sarmiento* of 1862. Alberdi and Sarmiento had
crossed swords over an adverse judgement that Alberdi made of
some poems which Sarmiento submitted to him for criticism;
but there was a fundamental difference of temperament between
the hot-headed *sanjuanino,* and the cool, supremely reasonable
jurist from Buenos Aires. Alberdi had some harsh things to say
about Sarmiento as a political figure, maintaining that he was
just as much a *caudillo* as Quiroga; and he was also uncompli-
mentary about his book, which he found structurally chaotic.
But the main criticism which he levels against him is that
Sarmiento is unaware of the political situation in Argentina, and
has failed to realise that money, not terror, was what kept Rosas
in power. This money came from the labour of the country, and
the labourer was the *gaucho,* whom Sarmiento condemned as a

barbarian, but who in fact represented European civilisation better than Sarmiento, dismissed by Alberdi as "trabajador improductivo, estéril, a título de empleado vitalicio, que vive como un doméstico de los salarios del Estado, su patrón". A republic which makes the civil service the most desirable form of livelihood is decadent and on the way to ruin, he goes on to say. Sarmiento was merely seeking to preserve the old system which depended on urban wealth, and might be described as *caudillaje letrado*. Alberdi pleads for greater provincial authority and independence *vis-à-vis* Buenos Aires, since the provinces are more progressive than the capital. He goes on to maintain that there was no need to make such an extensive appeal to social theory to account for the origin of an evildoer like Quiroga, for evildoers grow up like weeds, wherever there is a lack of authority to curb them, as there always had been in Argentina since the disappearance of the Spanish viceroys. Real power then fell into the hands of the wealthy, who were in the city rather than the country, where the true source of the country's wealth and civilisation lay. Sarmiento, as a man of the city, is seen as no less guilty than Quiroga of the evils from which Argentina was suffering.

This fundamental attack on Sarmiento's very *raison d'être,* as well as on the basic premisses of his *Facundo,* is one which must be taken seriously by those who come to *Facundo* as students of the history of Argentina; and moreover if it is to be admitted as just, it must to some extent throw seriously into question the validity of *Facundo* as a piece of historical and political writing. It does not however, it seems to me, really affect its importance as a sociological document or as a work of literature, and it is to the assessment of the work from these two points of view that we must now turn.

4. "Facundo" as a sociological document

In the *carta-prólogo* prefaced to the 1851 edition of *Facundo* Sarmiento had insisted that *Facundo* was not a history book, but a document for the future historian.[32] We have already had occasion to notice Manuel Gálvez's assertion that the author was primarily and always a journalist (*3*, 448). One of the most rewarding exercises of the journalist has become the preparation and presentation of documentaries, and it is perhaps as something between the political pamphlet and the modern documentary, with which we are more familiar nowadays through the media of cinema, radio and television, that we should most profitably approach *Facundo*.

Allison W. Bunkley, who has written one of the most useful books in English on Sarmiento, hints that in his book Sarmiento may have been a kind of pioneer in sociological method:

> Whatever the origin of the concept, the conflict between civilisation and barbarism became the essential problem that Don Domingo was studying. His interest was primarily to analyze the elements, the causes of each, in order to find a means for the triumph of the city and civilization. Sarmiento divided his study into two parts. First, he studied the environment and the effects that it had upon the problem. Second, he studied the human elements, the actors within the drama. Although the plan was carried out only in the most rudimentary form, it followed the general pattern that was later to become the basis of sociological analysis. Sarmiento did this some time before Taine had systematized the method, and he did it coincidentally with the innovations of Buckle and without previous knowledge of the Englishman's works. The originality of the method rather than the penetration of the study offers its most important claim to fame. . . .

---

32. "Facundo no es un libro de historia, sino un documento para el futuro historiador . . ." (quoted *10*, 65-6).

It was a simple task for Sarmiento to analyze the causes of barbarism. But for Sarmiento the reformer, it was necessary also to know how to replace the actual barbaric state with a civilized one. What would be the causes of civilization? He could not study the factors that contributed to it, for the civilization he aspired to did not exist. Since he had discarded *a priori* reasoning, this presented an interesting problem in method. Don Domingo resolved the difficulty by a negative analysis. He studied what was missing in the barbaric society. He reasoned that those factors missing in barbarism would be the factors that would cause civilization. The naive character of this method illustrates well the rudimentary stage at which the sociology of Sarmiento found itself at this time. (pp. 211-12)[33]

Sarmiento saw the causes of civilisation, lacking in Quiroga's province of La Rioja, as consisting in school, religion, houses, money, doctors, lawyers and judges. Instead there were *gauchos,* representing barbarism, and finding their prototypes in the local *caudillo* Quiroga and the national *caudillo* Rosas, each seen as the effect of material and racial causes.

How far Sarmiento intended *Facundo* as a sociological document or treatise, how far he would even have understood these terms, is very much open to question. His book remains, however, an interesting experiment in sociological method, even if it is now seen to be a very primitive and imperfect one. It is also seen as a piece of sociological theory which, open to attack as it has been and still is, may yet throw light on the history and present state of the various elements which go to make up the human structure of the Argentine Republic.[34]

33. Barrenechea, pointing out how before *Facundo* Sarmiento had seen the whole explanation for the plight of Argentina in the Spanish heritage, goes on: "Comparemos esto con la primera parte del *Facundo* donde analiza la influencia del suelo, el modo de colonización española, la distribución de las ciudades, las formas de sociabilidad que se establecieron, los tipos característicos que engendró lo hispánico trasladado al suelo y a las condiciones de vida americanas" (*13*, 204).

34. "Debe considerarse a Sarmiento, pues, aunque no como un constitucionalista de gran autoridad, al menos como al fundador de la sociología argentina. Aunque sus ideas no habrán sido nuevas y originales, desde el punto de vista de la ciencia universal, lo fueron ciertamente para su patria y pueblo, en la época en que escribía; . . ." C. O. Bunge, *Sarmiento (Estudio biográfico y crítico)*, Madrid, 1926, p. 199.

5. "Facundo" as a literary work

So far we have seen Sarmiento's *Facundo* as a political pamphlet, as a journalistic documentary and, in embryonic form, as a sociological study. It is perhaps fair to say at this stage that this is not the way in which the work is usually viewed, at least to begin with, by most of those who have dealt with it; and that for most students it is seen as a work of literature, by many critics even as an outstanding work of literature.[35] It is not my wish to dispute this traditional approach, but I think it is worth suggesting that *Facundo* is a literary work almost by accident. If we start from here it may in fact be easier to appreciate the literary qualities more fairly, as a bonus rather than as something we might justly expect to find.

Those who come to *Facundo* from the point of view of the literary critic are liable to be very disconcerted, even if not actually disappointed by what they find. It is almost impossible, to begin with, to classify the work, and any attempt to put it into a recognised literary genre is doomed to failure from the outset. Yet those who have expressed greatest appreciation of the book have seen in it the best features of several genres. The Argentinian poet Leopoldo Lugones, considered by many to be, next to Rubén Darío, the outstanding representative of *modernismo* in Spanish America, wrote a book on Sarmiento first published in 1911, which is as a whole a eulogy of the author.[36] Pointing out that *Facundo* was its author's first full-

35. Cf. A. Castro Leal, "El *Facundo* de Domingo Faustino Sarmiento" in *Cuadernos americanos,* IV, 5, 1945, p. 148: "Su mérito principal es, sin duda, un mérito literario. No quiero decir con esto que no tenga importancia — y la tiene muy grande — como documento para la historia política y social de la Argentina y, también, de la América española. Quiero señalar simplemente que su organización, su factura, el equilibrio de sus partes, la variedad de sus registros, su armonía y su contrapunto, todo aquello, en fin, por lo que vive para el público lector, lo debe al arte literario".

36. Not surprisingly, perhaps, since Lugones tells us himself: "porque se trata, ante todo, de glorificar a Sarmiento. Es éste el objeto del encargo que me ha dado el señor Presidente . . .", *Historia de Sarmiento,* Buenos Aires, 1931, p. 10.

length work, and indicating its origins as a pamphlet, he goes on to write : "Forzado por el calor febril, como una planta excesiva, aquel libro resultó una creación extraña, que participa de la historia, de la novela, de la política, del poema y del sermón" (p. 119).[37] A little later he goes on to say what the work meant for its author :

> El *Facundo* constituye todo el programa de Sarmiento. Sus ideas literarias, su propaganda política, sus planes de educador, su concepto histórico, están ahí. Es aquella nuestra gran novela política y nuestro gran estudio constitucional : una obra cíclica. El primer escritor argentino verdaderamente digno de este nombre había nacido. (p. 122)

Facundo is first and foremost, then, a hybrid work, with very little in the way of literary motivation. As we have seen, there is little evidence that Sarmiento had very much interest in literature except for the ideas it contained, although he did at one time try his hand at poetry and became involved in literary circles even to the extent of starting a literary society.[38] He had little time for established literary styles and movements, attacking neo-classicism as "mechanical imitation", and defining Romanticism as "writing for the sake of writing" (cf. *6*, 197). There are many features in his work which link him with the romantics, including the alleged titanism which has already been referred to;[39] and the one Spanish writer whom he truly admired was one who at least in some aspects of his work, and most aspects of his

---

37. Palcos writes : "*Facundo,* tal lo cierto, rompe con los moldes tradicionales de los géneros literarios. Clasificarlo, conforme se ha propuesto, entre las novelas, equivale a caer en error tan grave como incluirlo entre los libros de historia. *Facundo* es de todo un poco : biografía, novelesca por su interés, de Quiroga, y, en menor grado, de Rosas; magnífico poema descriptivo, hasta ahora no superado, de nuestra República y de los tipos peculiares que engendra; movida, dramática historia de la revolución y de los sucesos posteriores; fascinante ensayo sociológico trazado cuando el género está en pañales en Europa; . . . Finca su grandeza y su mucho brillo en la armoniosa fusión de tantos aspectos diversos y en la manera sagaz de realizarla. Libro-síntesis y libro-símbolo . . .

  "Una obra debe ser juzgada tal como es, no como el crítico quisiera que fuese . . ." (*10*, 67-8).
38. For an account of Sarmiento's literary activities, cf. *1,* chapter 7.
39. Cf. above p. 27.

life, was the Romantic *par excellence*. This was Larra, with whom Sarmiento has often been compared by critics. One writer, Luis Lorenzo-Rivero, has devoted a whole book to a comparison of the two authors.[40] Sarmiento maintained that Larra was the only Spanish writer ever read in America in his time; and he acknowledges his debt to Larra when he writes: " . . . no hemos visto allá [i.e., in America] más libro español que uno que no es libro: los artículos de periódico de Larra . . . "[41] The reference is to the articles now usually known as the *Artículos de costumbres,* which have given the name to a literary movement known as *costumbrismo,* a term which must be applied to some parts of *Facundo,* which many consider to be the best in the book, notably those descriptive of the various types of *gaucho* to be found in the Argentine *pampa.*[42]

This is another clue to the understanding and appreciation of Sarmiento's literary achievement in *Facundo.* His greatest admiration is expressed for a book which is not a book. We might legitimately infer from this that Sarmiento was not much concerned with orthodox genres or literary forms; and although we may still reasonably criticise *Facundo* for its formal imperfections, as many critics have done, it is not without significance that the author himself was probably not trying very hard in this direction. One ought perhaps to consider the question of the structure of the work at this stage, remembering once again that it appeared first of all in serial form in a newspaper.

The structure of "Facundo"

Facundo is divided into a fairly short introduction and into three parts of unequal length, the third being much shorter than the other two. The first part sets the scene, geographical and human, for the appearance of the main character in the work, Juan Facundo Quiroga, to whose life story and deeds the second and longest part of the book is devoted. The third part deals with

40. *Larra y Sarmiento*, Madrid, Guadarrama, 1968.

41. *Obras de Domingo Faustino Sarmiento*, Paris, 1889-1909, IV, p. 41. Sarmiento referred to Larra as the Cervantes of the regenerated Spain. ("Las obras de Larra", in *El Mercurio,* August 3, 1841, quoted *6,* 185). See *15,* 354.

42. Paul Verdevoye devotes a long chapter to the subject of *costumbrismo* (*1,* ch. 2).

the government of Rosas, and makes some generalisations about
the present and future of the Argentine Republic. This, at least,
is what one finds in most current editions of the book; but the
second and third editions, published in 1851 and 1868, lack the
last part. (The third edition, published in New York, contains
the preface to the English translation done by Mrs. Horace
Mann, as well as two other short works of Sarmiento.) In a letter
to his friend Valentín Alsina, he wrote:

> . . . He suprimido la introducción, como inútil, y los dos
> últimos capítulos como ociosos hoy, recordando una
> indicación de Vd. en 1846 en Montevideo, en que se
> insinuaba que el libro estaba terminado con la muerte de
> Quiroga. (quoted *10*, 52)

Alberto Palcos, in his book on *Facundo,* suggests that there were
other reasons for the changes made from the first edition; that
the horizons had cleared somewhat between 1845 and 1851, and
it was no longer tactful or so necessary to say the things which
he had said in the third part, and which he had justified power-
fully enough in presenting the first edition. Now, in the new
atmosphere of reconciliation, Sarmiento judged it better to
eliminate excuses for dissension. In the fourth edition of 1874,
published in Paris in the last year of Sarmiento's presidency, the
parts omitted were restored, so that, Palcos suggests, a comparison could be made between the plan for a new government
contained in the third part of *Facundo* and the achievements of
his own period of office. He would show in this way how far he
had remained faithful to his principles, even after thirty years.

Whether with or without the third part, *Facundo* has often
been criticised for the unevenness of its structure, and unity
has been alleged to exist not in the construction but in the
tone or the style.[43] It must be admitted that it is not always

43. Cf. E. Carilla, *Lengua y estilo en el Facundo*, Tucumán, 1954, p. 11. On
the other hand, P. Henríquez Ureña sees evidence of careful construction in
Facundo. He writes of Sarmiento's three best books, which include *Facundo*:
"Estan sólidamente construídos; los escribió de prisa, pero concibió su estructura íntegra y armoniosa desde el principio" (*Las corrientes literarias en la
América Hispánica*, Mexico-Buenos Aires, Fondo de Cultura Económica,
1949, p. 138). Cf. also *12*, 278-9.

easy to follow the course which Sarmiento sets for us in his book, and that there are sections of the work, especially in the second part where he is dealing with the life and deeds of Facundo Quiroga, which are bewildering and confusing to follow, and which are often frankly dull. One is led to and fro with no very clear idea of where one is going, or what is the point of going anyway. This second part, although one can see it as a logical sequel to the first part, and indeed as the only real excuse for the first part or for the whole book, is disappointing when one compares it with the lively and entertaining chapters describing the *gaucho* and his setting. The third part is again disconcerting, with its mixture of fierce condemnation of Rosas and his régime, and of visionary prophecies about the future of Argentina once he has been cleared out of the way. *Facundo* is good in parts; and one cannot help recalling Dr. Samuel Johnson's indignant rejoinder to Boswell about his reading practices: "No, Sir, do *you* read books *through*?"

The style of "Facundo"

Before going on to pick out the good bits, it is perhaps worth saying something in general about Sarmiento's style, although it is so varied that one will almost certainly find oneself coming to the same sort of conclusion about it as was reached earlier concerning the structure of *Facundo*. Again it is important to remember that Sarmiento did not care at all about aesthetic considerations for their own sake. Ana María Barrenechea, who has written on Sarmiento's style, has stated quite rightly that all his critics agree that he was never a pure creative writer, but a fighting author who took up the pen in defence of ideas. Sarmiento says as much himself, in the prologue to his *Campaña del Ejército Grande:* "Soldado, con la pluma o la espada, combato para poder escribir, que escribir es pensar; escribo como medio y arma de combate, que combatir es realizar el pensamiento" (quoted *12*, 275).

Sarmiento's anti-aesthetic ideas are nowhere more clearly in evidence than in the controversy in which he engaged with the Venezuelan statesman, scholar and poet Andrés Bello and his Chilean pupils, whom he advised in these vigorous terms:

Pero cambiad de estudios, y en lugar de ocuparos de las formas, de la pureza de las palabras, de lo redondeado de las frases, de lo que dijo Cervantes o Fray Luis de León, adquirid ideas de donde quiera que vengan, nutrid vuestro espíritu con las manifestaciones del pensamiento de los grandes luminares de la época; y cuando sintáis que vuestro pensamiento a su vez se despierta, echad miradas observadoras sobre vuestra patria, sobre el pueblo, las costumbres, las instituciones, las necesidades actuales, y en seguida escribid con amor, con corazón, lo que se os alcance, o que se os antoje, que eso será bueno en el fondo, aunque la forma sea incorrecta; será apasionado, aunque a veces sea inexacto; agradará al lector, aunque rabie Garcilaso; no se parecerá a lo de nadie; pero bueno o malo, será vuestro, nadie os lo disputará.[44]

One can understand how Sarmiento came to appeal to a writer like Miguel de Unamuno, who was convinced that it was much more important to have something to say than to say it elegantly and according to the rules.

Nevertheless – and in this he may be compared to Unamuno – Sarmiento's indifference to forms and traditions of style did not 'mean that he did not take care about his writing, in his own way and for his own reasons, just as he had been very deliberate in setting out the plan for *Facundo*. Sarmiento was well aware, as any orator or journalist is aware, of the power of words, and of how important it was to choose the right ones. Writing about Victor Hugo's play *Le Roi s'amuse*, he said : "El autor que en su obra deja que el fondo domine y sofoque a la forma, es impotente; y el que deja que la forma domine y sofoque al fondo, es charlatán . . . " (quoted *12, 277*).

At its best one can agree with Bunkley in saying that the style of *Facundo* is "a style whose beauty puts it at times in the category of prose-poetry. Sometimes it has a strong epic character in its descriptions; sometimes it demonstrates a marked lyricism . . . " (*6, 217*). It is clear that Sarmiento in this book, which he recognised as his masterpiece, took a great deal of

---

44. "Segunda contestación a un quidam", I, p. 223, quoted *12*, 276. It is perhaps worth pointing out that Sarmiento was, in spite of this observation, a great admirer of Cervantes.

trouble over the details of his writing. This can be seen from a
close comparison of the various early editions of *Facundo,* and
he even submitted the proofs of the third edition to the Cuban
grammarian Mantilla for his inspection and advice. He showed
himself surprisingly and unusually ready to listen to and act on
criticisms of this work (cf. *10*, 96).

For all his indifference to established norms on the one hand,
and his minute care over detail on the other, Sarmiento's style in
Facundo, like the structure of the book, leaves a final over-all
impression of unevenness. At his best, when he is evoking the
shade of Quiroga in the opening paragraph of his introduction,
or giving us what we might call the anatomy of the *gaucho,* he
is magnificent and carries us along willy-nilly. He is also a
splendid *raconteur,* and some of the stories told about Facundo
Quiroga are difficult to surpass; but against this one has to set
the rambling and often turgid accounts of the unending marches,
battles and campaigns which Quiroga waged, where Sarmiento
seems to have been abandoned by all his poetic, narrative and
analytical powers, and where, we are told, even the facts are
wrong and hopelessly distorted.[45] We shall have to return to the
question of Sarmiento's historical accuracy later;[46] but the time
has come to look at the text of *Facundo* in a little more detail
than we have done so far.

---

45. Admittedly the allegation is made by a hostile critic, Manuel Gálvez (*3*, 460).
46. See below pp. 60-63.

6. The introduction to "Facundo"

As with all the chapters of his book, Sarmiento heads his introduction with a quotation. The nature as well as the content of these quotations is very revealing. The one here comes from Villemain's *Cours de littérature française* of 1828, a work which, scarcely widely known nowadays, has been described as a pioneering work of the kind of literary criticism which takes account of social influences as well as those of other literatures, and requires of the critic that he be a good writer himself.[47] Sarmiento's range of authors chosen for these introductory quotations is very wide, and shows the catholicity of thought and taste which we might expect. He does not mind whether he quotes them in the original language or in translation, provided they supply grist for his mill; and he is not careful to give full references: here for instance he refers simply to "Villemain, 'Cours de Littérature' ". It is well worth looking at these quotations, which tell us a good deal, even if very briefly, about the author's views. This one, for instance, is very enlightening about Sarmiento's attitude to history: "Je demande à l'historien l'amour de l'humanité ou de la liberté; sa justice impartiale ne doit être impassible. Il faut, au contraire, qu'il espère, qu'il souffre, ou soit heureux de ce qu'il raconte." This will not be without significance when we come to consider the historicity of Sarmiento's work.

The introduction itself opens with a splendid piece of oratory, in which the shade of Facundo is evoked:

¡Sombra terrible de Facundo, voy a evocarte, para que, sacudiendo el ensangrentado polvo que cubre tus cenizas, te levantes a explicarnos la vida secreta y las convulsiones internas que desgarran las entrañas de un noble pueblo! Tú posees el secreto, ¡revélanoslo! Diez años aun después de tu trágica muerte, el hombre de las ciudades y el gaucho

47. Cf. E. Abry, C. Audic, P. Crouzet, *Histoire illustrée de la littérature française*, Paris, 1926, p. 641.

de los llanos argentinos, al tomar diversos senderos en el
desierto, decían: "¡No! ¡no ha muerto! ¡Vive aún! ¡El
vendrá!" . . . (p. 1a).

It is a little surprising to find Sarmiento referring to the
"trágica muerte" of Facundo, although of course it does fore-
shadow the admiration which the author is to show throughout
the book for things which he formally and officially disapproves
of and condemns – such as barbarism and the *gaucho*.[48] The fact
that Facundo is a spectre, to be contrasted with the deadly cold
present reality of Rosas, hints at an explanation of why Sarmiento has chosen to write about a dead local *caudillo* when
he is really concerned with attacking the much more dangerous
national *caudillo* who is all too much alive. It is through studying
Facundo and his background that Sarmiento will lead his readers
to an understanding of the phenomenon of the social reality of
the Argentine Republic, which has had no de Tocqueville to
analyse it. Whether Sarmiento sees himself in the role of this
famous French historian and sociologist who dissected the body
politic of the United States is not clear, but the appearance of
La Démocratie en Amérique in 1835 was recent enough to invite
comparison.[49] Where Sarmiento breaks new ground is in presenting his country in terms of a person. In a later study than the
one already mentioned on Sarmiento's style, Ana María
Barrenechea has examined the ideas of the author before the
publication of *Facundo,* and has suggested that pedagogical
reasons led him to use this form of approach to history through
biography. Sarmiento wrote an article under the title "De las
biografías", published in *El Mercurio* on 20 May 1842, in which
he expressed the view that it is easier to interest the common
reader in a historical period, and for him to understand it,
through the person of a man who reflects it. Also, as Sarmiento
affirms in the same article, there are aesthetic and personal
reasons, for the biographer has the pleasure of the literary
creator who feels like a god making creatures out of air. And,

48. Cf. the Preface, above.
49. Verdevoye writes of Sarmiento: "Sa façon d'envisager l'histoire en fait donc
    un disciple de Tocqueville, de Guizot et de Michelet, qu'il admire et qu'il
    mentionne fréquemment" (*1*, 381).

finally, the interest in biography reflects the constant and dominating interest in humanity which breathes through the whole of Sarmiento's work. Having no taste for abstract thought, Sarmiento always preferred to clothe it in living concrete forms (*13*, esp. 197-8). Again one is reminded of Unamuno, and at the same time made aware that Sarmiento could scarcely have been a de Tocqueville even if he had wanted to.

7. Primera parte

(A) The physical background and the people.

A straightforward geographical description soon focuses on what is to be at the root of Sarmiento's thought, the contrast between the city and the country. Of the two cities situated on the River Plate, Montevideo and Buenos Aires, the latter "está llamada a ser un día la ciudad más gigantesca de ambas Américas", even though as he writes barbarism and violence have descended upon it, and it is incapable of transmitting the progressive civilisation which is its natural heritage to the rest of the country, cut off by the *pampa*. The city is inhabited by descendants of Andalusian soldiers and foreign immigrants, while the *pampas,* as Sarmiento has it on the authority of no less a person than Sir Walter Scott, whom Sarmiento later refers to as "el buen *gringo*", "no están pobladas sino por cristianos salvajes conocidos bajo el nombre de *huachos* (por decir *gauchos*), cuyo principal amueblado consiste en cráneos de caballos, cuyo alimento es carne cruda y agua, y cuyo pasatiempo favorito es reventar caballos en carreras forzadas".[50] These different groups are distinguished by their very different forms of dress:

> *El hombre de la ciudad viste el traje europeo,* vive de la vida civilizada tal como la conocemos en todas partes; allí están las leyes, las ideas de progreso, los medios de instrucción, alguna organización municipal, el gobierno regular, etc. Saliendo del recinto de la ciudad, todo cambia de aspecto; *el hombre de campo lleva otro traje que llamaré americano,* por ser común a todos los pueblos; sus hábitos de vida son diversos, sus necesidades peculiares y limitadas; parecen dos sociedades distintas, dos pueblos extraños uno de otro. Aún hay más; el hombre de la campaña, lejos de aspirar a semejarse al de la ciudad, rechaza con desdén su lujo y sus modales corteses; y el vestido del ciudadano, el frac, la capa, la silla,

50. Sarmiento had translated novels of Sir Walter Scott when he worked in the mines in Chile.

ningún signo europeo puede presentarse impunemente en la campaña. Todo lo que hay de civilizado en la ciudad está bloqueado por allí, proscrito afuera; y el que osara mostrarse con levita, por ejemplo, y montado en silla inglesa atraería sobre sí las burlas y las agresiones brutales de los campesinos. (p. 16b)

Sarmiento clearly takes his stand with the city-dwellers and their civilised habits and forms of dress. It is interesting that he always carefully cultivated this kind of dress himself, and that when he joined the army he had himself made and always wore the full uniform of a French officer.[51] It is clear that Sarmiento takes as his official position one of scorn towards the countryman, whom he equates a little later on with the primitive tribesmen of Asia in Biblical times: "La vida primitiva de los pueblos, la vida eminentemente bárbara y estacionaria, la vida de Abrahán, que es la del beduino de hoy, asoma en los campos argentinos, aunque modificada por la civilización de un modo extraño" (p. 17a). Christianity exists, but is merely a traditional hangover, like the Spanish language, "que se perpetúa, pero corrompido, encarnado en supersticiones groseras, sin instrucción, sin culto y sin convicciones" (p. 19a).

Oddly enough, these assertions follow a description of a scene which obviously moved Sarmiento considerably, and which portrays a patriarch leading the family devotions, in the heart of the country and far from the ministrations of any priest. This curious inconsistency, as it must strike the reader, paves the way for one of the most worrying features of Sarmiento's book, the treatment of the *gaucho*.

(B) The gaucho.

Among the claims made for *Facundo* is that of being the first work of what has been called *literatura gauchesca*, or literature concerning the *gaucho* or Argentine herdsman.[52] This is a well-

51. On the importance which Sarmiento attached to dress cf. *1*, 394-5. Cf. also David Viñas, *Literatura argentina y realidad política de Sarmiento a Cortázar*, Buenos Aires, Ediciones Siglo Veinte, 1971, 168-9.
52. In a sense, the claim is implicit in something which Sarmiento himself wrote shortly after the publication of *Facundo*, in a letter from Montevideo to Vicente Fidel López, quoted by N. Salomon, *15*, 344.

known sub-genre in Latin-American literature, which in effect crosses the normal literary genre divisions. The bulk of *gaucho* literature is in fact poetry of a more or less epic type, the masterpiece being José Hernández's *Martín Fierro* of 1874 and its sequel *La vuelta de Martín Fierro*. One may also include in this subgenre the plays of Florencio Sánchez, and at least one modern novel which has achieved world fame, and has been translated for the Penguin series, Ricardo Güiraldes's *Don Segundo Sombra*. Although the treatment of the *gaucho* varies considerably in the various works of literature in which he has appeared during a period of almost a century (*Don Segundo Sombra* dates from 1926), he is most characteristically presented as an outsider, even if not as an outlaw; but as a curiously appealing outsider, in a way which strikes one as rather modern – although of course one can point to the *pícaro* as representing the same phenomenon.

Sarmiento's attitude to the *gaucho* is a very strange one. As a man who stood for civilisation as against barbarism, for the city against the country, for education against ignorance, for progress against tradition, one might have expected the author of *Facundo* to disapprove of the *gaucho* and all that he stood for. In a sense, formally and officially, he does so; and yet we have in this work one of the most understanding and sympathetic, even admiring, pictures of the Argentine cowboy that one can find anywhere. Almost totally lacking education, the *gaucho* boy enters a life of independence, and one which has no regular occupation of any kind. Sarmiento writes :

Aquí principia la vida pública, diré del gaucho, pues que su educación está ya terminada. Es preciso ver a estos españoles, por el idioma únicamente y por las confusas nociones religiosas que conservan, para saber apreciar los caracteres indómitos y altivos que nacen de esta lucha del hombre aislado con la naturaleza salvaje, el racional con el bruto; es preciso ver estas caras cerradas de barba, estos semblantes graves y serios, como los de los árabes asiáticos, para juzgar del compasivo desdén que les inspira la vista del hombre sedentario de las ciudades, que puede haber leído muchos libros, pero que no sabe aterrar un toro bravío y darle muerte, que no sabrá proveerse de caballo a campo abierto, a pie y sin auxilio

de nadie, nunca ha parado un tigre, recibiéndolo con el puñal
en una mano y el poncho envuelto en la otra, para meterlo
en el hocico mientras le traspasa el corazón y lo deja tendido a
sus pies. Este hábito de triunfar de las resistencias, de mostrarse siempre superior a la naturaleza, de desafiarla y ven-
cerla, desenvuelve prodigiosamente el sentimiento de la importancia individual y de la superioridad. Los argentinos, de
cualquier clase que sean, civilizados o ignorantes, tienen una
alta conciencia de su valer como nación; todos los demás
pueblos americanos los echan en cara esta vanidad, y se
muestran ofendidos en su presunción y arrogancia. Creo que
el cargo no es del todo infundado, y no me pesa de ello. ¡Ay
del pueblo que no tiene fe en sí mismo! ¡Para ése no se han
hecho las grandes cosas! ¿Cuánto no habrá podido contribuir
a la independencia de una parte de la América la arrogancia
de estos gauchos argentinos, que nadie ha visto el sol mejor
que ellos, ni el hombre sabio ni el poderoso? El europeo es
para ellos el último de todos, porque no resiste a un par de
corcovos del caballo. Si el origen de esta vanidad nacional en
las clases inferiores es mezquino, no son por eso menos nobles
las consecuencias, como no es menos pura el agua de un río
porque nazca de vertientes cenagosas e infectas . . .
    La vida del campo, pues, ha desenvuelto en el gaucho las
facultades físicas, sin ninguna de las de la inteligencia . . .
    (pp. 19b-20a)

This important passage does a good deal to explain the ambi-
valent attitude which runs through *Facundo*, especially in con-
nection with the presentation of the *gaucho* as the symbol of
barbarism. It opens the way into what is probably the most
striking and in some ways the most important part of the book,
at least from the literary point of view. Chapter II of the first part
of the book, with its title "Originalidad y caracteres argentinos.
El rastreador. El baquiano. El gaucho malo. El cantor," presents
us with what might be called an anatomy of the *gaucho*, fascinating in itself and as an example of excellent writing in the *costumbrista* manner, but also significant in that, within the categories
isolated by Sarmiento we have, he claims, the basic features of the
gaucho type which will recur again and again in the *caudillos*
who intervene in the life of the Argentine Republic.

In introducing his detailed picture of *gaucho* types, Sarmiento
has incidentally marked out one of the features which for a long
time was to distinguish the literature of Latin America as a whole
from that of its European forebears, the attention to the countryside. He has also defined one of the themes which have reap-
peared many times in the literature of the subcontinent, the
struggle between civilisation and barbarism, a theme which
underlies another of the great works which has been the subject
of one of the critical guides in this present series, *Doña Bárbara*,
by the Venezuelan Rómulo Gallegos.[53] Near the beginning of this
second chapter Sarmiento writes :

> Si un destello de literatura nacional puede brillar momentá-
> neamente en las nuevas sociedades americanas, es el que
> resultará de la descripción de las grandiosas escenas naturales,
> y sobre todo de la lucha entre la civilización europea y la
> barbarie indígena, entre la inteligencia y la materia; la lucha
> imponente en América, y que da lugar a escenas tan pecu-
> liares, tan características y tan fuera del círculo de ideas en
> que se ha educado el espíritu europeo, porque los resortes
> dramáticos se vuelven desconocidos fuera del país donde se
> toman, los usos sorprendentes y originales los caracteres.
> (p. 21a).

Sarmiento notes how similarities of background tend to produce
the same kind of characters and the same literary manifestations.
He mentions Fenimore Cooper, and especially *The Last of the
Mohicans*, which is known to have influenced his work, and
which again invites attention for those who are interested in
the exercise of comparative literature.[54] As well as a number of
specific examples, says Sarmiento :

> mil otros accidentes que omito, prueban la verdad de que
> modificaciones análogas del suelo traen análogas costumbres,
> recursos y expedientes. No es otra la razón de hallar en Feni-
> more Cooper descripciones de usos y costumbres que parecen
> plagiadas de la pampa; . . . (p. 22a).

53. Cf. D. L. Shaw, *Gallegos: Doña Bárbara*, London, Grant & Cutler, 1972.
54. Cf. P. Verdevoye, op. cit., p. 383. Cf. also D. S. Vivian, "The protagonist
    in the works of Sarmiento and Cooper", *Hispania* (U.S.A.), xlviii, 1965, pp.
    806-10.

The product of the natural character of the country and the exceptional customs it engenders is, says Sarmiento, a kind of poetry. This view of poetry as the product of an imaginative contemplation of Nature is an essentially Romantic one. In the case of Sarmiento the imagination must have played a large part in his appreciation of the poetry, for, as we have noted before, at the time he wrote *Facundo* the author had never seen the *pampa*, about whose effect in stirring up poetic creation he writes at length :

Ahora yo pregunto : ¿qué impresiones ha de dejar en el habitante de la República Argentina el simple acto de clavar los ojos en el horizonte, y ver . . . no ver nada? Porque cuanto más se hunde los ojos en aquel horizonte incierto, vaporoso, indefinido, más se aleja, más lo fascina, lo confunde y lo sume en la contemplación y la duda. ¿Dónde termina aquel mundo que quiere en vano penetrar? ¡No lo sabe! ¿Qué hay más allá de lo que se ve? La soledad, el peligro, el salvaje, la muerte. He aquí ya la poesía. El hombre que se mueve en estas escenas, se siente asaltado de temores e incertidumbres fantásticas, de sueños que le preocupan despierto. (p. 22b).

So the Argentine people are poets, almost willy-nilly; and they are musicians too, whether in the cultured or the popular manner. Clearly Sarmiento is more interested in the popular tradition, in the music most usually consisting of songs accompanied by the lute (*vihuela*) or the guitar; and he gives us a summary of the main kinds of *gaucho* songs, with their characteristics and the circumstances to which they are most suited : the *triste*, the *vidalita*, the popular metre used for commenting on everyday events and for warsongs; the *cielito*.

This is the way into Sarmiento's sketches of the four main types of *gaucho*, the *rastreador* or tracker, the *baquiano* or pathfinder, the *gaucho malo* or outlaw, and the *cantor* or minstrel. Here undoubtedly we have Sarmiento at his best and most vivid and compelling as a writer. Here he combines brilliance of descriptive and narrative skill with a precise and compelling choice of words, a word order, balance and flow which would be hard to surpass. We must agree that the most extraordinary of the *gaucho* types is the *rastreador*, whose gifts are nothing short of uncanny. Of one of these trackers, known as Calíbar, whom the author did not himself know, he relates that once when he was absent on a visit to Buenos Aires his show harness (*montura de gala*) was stolen. We read on :

> Su mujer tapó el rastro con una artesa. Dos meses después Calíbar regresó, vio el rastro ya borrado e imperceptible para otros ojos, y no se habló más del caso. Año y medio después Calíbar marcha cabizbajo por una calle de los suburbios, entra en una casa, y encuentra su montura ennegrecida ya, casi inutilizada por el uso. ¡Había encontrado el rastro de su raptor después de dos años! (p. 25a).

Similar stories are told about all the other types; and it will be remembered that Sarmiento made the claim that all the *caudillos* belonged to one or other of the *gaucho* patterns, even if, as in the case of Rosas, he was a *gaucho* only as it were by adoption. So Sarmiento illustrates his account of the *baquiano* (pathfinder) by mentioning that Rosas could tell by its taste the grass from every *estancia* in the south Buenos Aires province.

The *gaucho malo* or outlaw is important in that he is at the same time a figure with clear literary precedents and parallels, and the type to which Facundo Quiroga, the subject of Sarmiento's book, belonged :

> El *Gaucho Malo*, este es un tipo de ciertas localidades, un *outlaw*, un *squatter*, un misántropo particular. Es el *Ojo del Halcón*, el *Trampero* de Cooper, con toda su ciencia del desierto, con toda su aversión a las poblaciones de los blancos; pero sin su moral natural y sin sus conexiones con los salvajes. Llámanle el *Gaucho Malo*, sin que este epíteto le desfavorezca del todo. La justicia lo persigue desde muchos años; su nombre es temido, pronunciado en voz baja, pero sin odio y casi con respeto . . . (p. 27a).

It is clear that whatever his reputation, as far as Sarmiento is concerned, the *gaucho malo* is the type who has least to be said in his favour.

On the other hand, the *cantor* comes as near as one could expect to being idealised by the author of *Facundo*. What Sarmiento tells us about him and his songs is interesting and valuable, among other reasons because of its relevance to the *poesía gauchesca* which was to flourish in Argentina from the time of Hilario Ascasubi until it reached its high point in *Martín Fierro*; and of which we are already given some idea in the eighteenth-century *Lazarillo de ciegos caminantes* of the author known as "*Concolorcorvo*". Sarmiento's description of the *gaucho cantor* has become a classic :

El cantor. Aquí tenéis la idealización de aquella vida de revueltas, de civilización, de barbarie y de peligros. El gaucho cantor es el mismo bardo, el vate, el trovador de la Edad Media, que se mueve en la misma escena, entre las luchas de las ciudades y del feudalismo de los campos, entre la vida que se va y la vida que se acerca. El cantor anda de pago en pago, "de tapera en galpón", cantando sus héroes de la pampa perseguidos por la justicia, los llantos de la viuda a quien los indios robaron sus hijos en un malón reciente, la derrota y la muerte del valiente Rauch, la catástrofe de Facundo Quiroga y la suerte que cupo a Santos Pérez. El cantor está haciendo candorosamente el mismo trabajo de crónica, costumbres, historias, biografía, que el bardo de la Edad Media, y sus versos serían recogidos más tarde como los documentos y datos en que habría de apoyarse el historiador futuro, si a su lado no estuviese otra sociedad culta con superior inteligencia de los acontecimientos, que la que el infeliz despliega en sus rapsodias ingenuas. (p. 28a).

Just as the *gaucho cantor* is an important figure in the way in which he at once looks back to the medieval ballad-singer, and forward to the *poeta gauchesco*, so the description of his songs has comparative as well as intrinsic interest :

Por lo demás, la poesía original del cantor es pesada, monótona, irregular, cuando se abandona a la inspiración del momento. Más narrativa que sentimental, llena de imágenes tomadas de la vida campestre, del caballo y de las escenas del desierto, que la hacen metafórica y pomposa. Cuando refiere sus proezas o las de algún afamado malévolo, parécese al improvisador napolitano, desarreglado, prosaico de ordinario,

elevándose a la altura poética por momentos, para caer de
nuevo al recitado insípido y casi sin versificación. Fuera de
esto, el cantor posee su repertorio de poesías populares, quin-
tillas, décimas y octavas, diversos géneros de versos octosí-
labos. Entre éstos hay muchas composiciones de mérito, que
descubren inspiración y sentimiento. (p. 29ab)

In concluding his account of the four kinds of *gaucho,*
Sarmiento is careful to remind us of their relevance to the overall
plan of his book, telling us that we will be able to pick out and
recognise all of them as he unfolds the story of the Argentine
Republic in the age of the *caudillos,* men who have terrorised
their country and whose fame has often spread out into the world
outside.

Although this claim has some truth in it, and we are certainly
reminded later in the work that Facundo is the embodiment
of the *gaucho malo,* many of those who have studied Sarmiento's
work have remarked on two aspects of these sketches of the
four types of *gaucho* : the obvious exaggeration which they contain; and the elements of *costumbrismo.* Exaggeration is in fact
one of the faults towards which Sarmiento was disposed, and it
is one which we shall have to bear in mind when we come to
consider the historicity of his work, particularly in the second
part where he traces the life and deeds of Facundo. But the
exaggeration of these sketches is of the type which is associated
with the phenomenon known as *costumbrismo.*[55]

We have already seen that Sarmiento was a great admirer of
Larra, the most famous of the Peninsular *costumbrista* writers.
Luis Lorenzo-Rivero, in the book on Larra and Sarmiento which
I have mentioned earlier, has compared the views of the two
authors on a number of similar or parallel subjects, and has also
made a study of their styles which shows up a number of
resemblances. Sarmiento, in a letter to Vicente Fidel López
from Montevideo shortly after the publication of *Facundo,* writes
as follows :

    Echeverría describiendo las escenas de la pampa;
    Maldonado imitando el llano lenguaje lleno de imágenes

55. Cf. above pp. 35-6.

campestres del cantor; ¡qué diablos! ¿por qué no he de
decirlo? yo intentando describir en Quiroga la vida, los
instintos del pastor argentino, y Rugendas pintando con
verdad las costumbres americanas: he aquí los comienzos
de aquella literatura fantástica, homérica de la vida bárbara
del gaucho . . .

The French scholar Noël Salomon, who quotes this letter
(*15*, 344), and who refers to the allegation that Sarmiento made
that there was only one Spanish book in America, and that not
really a book – Larra's newspaper articles – has suggested that
the portrait of the *rastreador* may well have been done already as
an article before Sarmiento conceived clearly the idea of incor-
porating it in his anti-Rosas pamphlet. He points out how the
sketches of the four *gaucho* types are of more or less equal length,
and that it is the length of an average *artículo de costumbres* by
Larra. He in fact mentions Larra's *El zapatero viejo* of 1836 and
makes a comparison of the technique used here and by Sarmiento
in the piece on the *gaucho baquiano* (*15*, 365). He also points to
precedents in the essays of the English writers Steele and
Addison, and for the theory of the type as the key to the understanding of history he mentions the parallel with Balzac's
Comédie humaine, as well as a number of others, which include
once again Fenimore Cooper. A few years ago in this country
a number of books appeared which had as their title "The, or
An, Anatomy of this, that or the other". It appears that in the
1840's a similar vogue existed of writing books on the Physiology
of various phenomena or institutions, for example that of
marriage, and that these were often a kind of synthesis of
smaller sketches written earlier and then put together for a
larger publication (cf. *15*, 383).

It would not be right to see *Facundo* as either a collection
of *costumbrista* articles or as an anatomy, or physiology, of the
gaucho; but the portraits of the various type of *gaucho* in
chapter two of the first part of Sarmiento's book are certainly
in the *costumbrista* tradition, and could have been written earlier
and then incorporated in a work which to some extent shares the
documentary approach of the "Anatomy" kind of book.

The *costumbrista* note is continued in the third chapter of the first part of *Facundo*, in which the habits and setting of the *gaucho* are described. The idle existence of the *gaucho*, who leaves all work to his womenfolk, is largely filled with riding horses; and the horse becomes such an essential part of the *gaucho*'s existence that to be without one is hardly to live at all. So the story is told of a *caudillo* who emigrated to Chile, and when asked how he was: "¡Cómo me ha de ir! – contestó con el acento del dolor y la melancolía, ¡en Chile y a pie!" (p. 30b). In the aimless existence which is the *gaucho*'s heritage drink becomes a means of stirring the imagination into life, and the *pulpería*, the store from which liquor is obtained, becomes the social centre of the *gaucho*'s existence. Fighting becomes a regular feature of living, but for the sake of passing the time rather than for killing, which is looked upon with horror. The *gaucho*, caught up in the purposeless round of his life on the *pampas*, becomes either a criminal or a *caudillo*, engaging first of all in warfare and then in politics: "Es singular que todos los caudillos de la revolución argentina han sido comandantes de campaña: López e Ibarra, Artigas y Güemes, Facundo y Rosas" (p. 33a).

(C) The Revolution of 1810.

Such then are the physical and the human settings for the rising against the Spanish colonial authorities which took place in 1810. There were two distinct societies, incompatible rivals in Argentina before 1810: one Spanish, European, civilised; the other barbarous, American, almost indigenous. The revolution of 1810 was a revolution of the cities, which replaced one white urban oligarchy by another; and the consequence, as far as the situation of the Argentine population was concerned, was to bring the European and the native American societies into conflict more than ever, the end result being the absorption of the one by the other, the civilised society by the forces of barbarism, so that a Facundo could triumph and make way for "el gobierno central unitario, despótico, del estanciero don Juan Manuel de Rosas, que clava en la culta Buenos Aires el cuchillo del gaucho y destruye la obra de los siglos, la civilización, las leyes y la libertad" (p. 34b).

This, as far as Sarmiento is concerned, is the real beginning of his story, for which what he has written so far is a kind of preface. The reader will be forgiven if he judges this very long preface as the most interesting, well-written and important part of the book, and the one which has the most lasting value. It is, of course, of interest to know that Artigas, the first of the *caudillos* to gain extensive power in the provinces, represents the type of the *gaucho baquiano* of Sarmiento's 'Anatomy of the *gaucho*', making war on the cities; but the results of his successes represent disaster for Argentina, for whose provinces two centuries will not suffice to restore them to the paths of civilisation which they have abandoned. The closing words of the first part of *Facundo* sound ominously:

Dos siglos no bastarán para volverlas al camino que han abandonado, desde que la generación presente educa a sus hijos en la barbarie que a ella la ha alcanzado. Pregúntasenos ahora: ¿por qué combatimos? Combatimos por volver a las ciudades su vida propia. (p. 42b)

8. Segunda parte

The second, by far the longest, and in many ways the least interesting of the three parts of *Facundo,* is to a large extent a straightforward "Life and Works" study of a not very obviously important *gaucho* leader whose main appeal lies in his symbolic significance as the representative of what Sarmiento considered to be the barbarism of the class to which he belonged, and of the country from which he came and where he chiefly operated. Once again, a clue is provided for the significance of the narrative by the quotations which Sarmiento places at the head of the chapters, often taken from what would seem to be the most unlikely sources. The first chapter of this second part of *Facundo,* entitled "Infancia y juventud de Juan Facundo Quiroga", has a passage in French from the *Histoire de l'Empire Ottoman* of Alix, which makes clear to us what Sarmiento is trying to prove as he tells us the life story of Facundo Quiroga. "Au surplus, ces traits appartiennent au caractère original du genre humain. L'homme de la nature et qui n'a pas encore appris à contenir ou déguiser ses passions, les montre dans toute leur énergie et se libre à toute leur impétuosité" (p. 45). In other words, we are being told the story not of "l'homme moyen sensuel", but of the primitive, savage barbarian, the Tiger of the Plains, as he was to be known. The portrait which follows this is one which is heavily weighted towards this preconceived idea, accepting the view that man's appearance and resemblance to that of certain animals are indications of his character and aptitudes :

Facundo, pues, era de estatura baja y fornida, sus anchas espaldas sostenían sobre un cuello corto una cabeza bien formada, cubierta de pelo espesísimo, negro y ensortijado. Su cara, poco ovalada, estaba hundida en medio de un bosque de pelo, a que correspondía una barba igualmente crespa y negra, que subía hasta los pómulos bastante pronunciados para descubrir una voluntad firme y tenaz.
Sus ojos negros, llenos de fuego y sombreados por pobladas

cejas, causaban una sensación involuntaria de terror en
aquellos en quienes alguna vez llegaban a fijarse, porque
Facundo no miraba nunca de frente, y por hábito, por arte,
por deseo de hacerse siempre temible, tenía de ordinario
la cabeza siempre inclinada, y miraba por entre las cejas,
como el Alí-Bajá de Montvoisin. El Caín que representa la
famosa compañía Ravel, me despierta la imagen de Quiroga,
quitando las posiciones artísticas de la estatuaria que no le
convienen. Por lo demás, su fisonomía era regular, y el pálido
moreno de su tez sentaba bien a las sombras espesas en que
quedaba encerrada.

La estructura de su cabeza revelaba, sin embargo, bajo
esta cubierta selvática, la organización privilegiada de los
hombres nacidos para mandar. Quiroga poseía esas cualidades
naturales que hicieron del estudiante de Brienne el genio de
la Francia, y del mameluco oscuro que se batía con los
franceses en las Pirámides, el virrey de Egipto. La sociedad
en que nacen da a esos caracteres la manera especial de
manifestarse; sublimes, clásicos, por decirlo así, van al frente
de la humanidad civilizada, en unas partes, terribles,
sanguinarios y malvados, son en otras su mancha, su oprobio.
(pp. 46b-47a)

This fairly orthodox piece of portraiture is followed by an
account of Facundo's origins and upbringing. The son of a
humble *sanjuanino,* and therefore by birth a compatriot of
Sarmiento himself, he receives an education of the most rudimentary kind, and already reveals the ruthless and unscrupulous
violence of the future *caudillo.* Sarmiento recalls how one of his
schoolmasters, tired of dealing with his uncontrollable character,
provided himself with a new whip which he showed to the
terrified children, whom he told that he was going to try it out
on Facundo. Facundo, at the time a boy of just over eleven
years old, heard the threat and decided to put it to the test the
following day. The anecdote goes on:

No sabe la lección, pero pide al maestro que se la tome en
persona porque el pasante le quiere mal. El maestro
condesciende; Facundo comete un error, comete dos, tres,
cuatro; entonces el maestro hace uso del látigo; y Facundo,
que todo lo ha calculado, hasta la debilidad de la silla en que

su maestro está sentado, dale una bofetada, vuélcalo de
espaldas, y entre el alboroto que esta escena suscita, toma
la calle y va a esconderse entre ciertos parrones de una viña,
de donde no se le saca sino después de tres días. ¿No es ya el
caudillo que va a desafiar más tarde a la sociedad entera?
(p. 47b),

asks Sarmiento. Ill-educated as he is, Facundo deliberately
chooses to live at a lower level than that to which he has been
brought up, and allows his instincts and passions full reign. His
violence anticipates that of a character created by our contem-
porary novelist Camilo José Cela in his first novel *La familia de
Pascual Duarte*. A compulsive gambler, Facundo on one occasion lost a whole year's salary in one bet, and as he strode silently
off, he was stopped by a judge, who asked him to produce what
would be the equivalent of his employment card (*su papeleta de
conchavo*). The story goes on:

> Facundo aproximó su caballo en ademán de entregársela,
> afectó buscar algo en su bolsillo, y dejó tendido al juez de
> una puñalada. ¿Se vengaba en el juez de la reciente pérdida?
> ¿Quería sólo saciar el encono de gaucho malo contra la
> autoridad civil y añadir este nuevo hecho al brillo de su
> naciente fama? Lo uno y lo otro. Estas venganzas sobre el
> primer objeto que se presentaba, son frecuentes en su vida.
> Cuando se apellidaba general y tenía coroneles a sus órdenes,
> hacía dar en su casa en San Juan doscientos azotes a uno de
> ellos por haberle ganado mal, decía; a un joven doscientos
> azotes por haberse permitido una chanza en momentos en
> que él no estaba para chanzas; a una mujer de Mendoza que
> le había dicho al paso "adiós, mi general", cuando él iba
> enfurecido porque no había conseguido intimidar a un
> vecino tan pacífico, tan juicioso, como era valiente y gaucho,
> doscientos azotes. (p. 48b)

The anecdotes told about Facundo are legion, and Sarmiento
assures us that he has omitted many, aiming simply to show what
kind of man this local tyrant was, and thereby the nature of the
caudillos who succeeded in stifling the civilisation of the cities.
What is curious is that even when he is diagnosing the ills of his

country and attributing them to these representatives of violence,
he cannot conceal the fact that he sees in Quiroga not a petty
villain but a great man. Perverse and irreligious, believing in
nothing and determined to inspire fear, nevertheless for
Sarmiento

> Toda la vida pública de Quiroga me parece resumida en
> estos datos. Veo en ellos el hombre grande, el hombre genio,
> a su pesar, sin saberlo él, el César, el Tamerlán, el Mahoma.
> Ha nacido así y no es culpa suya; se bajará en las escalas
> sociales para mandar, para dominar, para combatir el poder
> de la ciudad, la partida de la policía. ¡Si le ofrecen una
> plaza en los ejércitos, la desdeñará, porque no tiene paciencia
> para aguardar los ascensos, porque hay mucha sujeción,
> muchas trabas puestas a la independencia individual; hay
> generales que pesan sobre él, hay una casaca que oprime el
> cuerpo y una táctica que regla los pasos; ¡todo esto es
> insufrible! ... (p. 51a)

He is the natural man, the creature of instinct, the epitome of
violence and savagery, capable of the most inhuman repulsive
cruelty, and yet, victim of determinist forces, he is nevertheless
the possessor of a sort of Salomonic wisdom, about which a whole
collection of anecdotes is also related, several of which are told
by Sarmiento in a way which reveals the skilled teacher and
raconteur. "¿Qué diferencia hay", he asks,

> entre aquel famoso expediente de mandar partir en dos el
> niño disputado, a fin de descubrir la verdadera madre, y este
> otro para encontrar un ladrón? Entre los individuos que
> formaban una compañía, habíase robado un objeto, y todas
> las diligencias practicadas para descubrir al raptor habían
> sido infructuosas. Quiroga forma la tropa, hace cortar tantas
> varitas de igual tamaño cuantos soldados había; hace en
> seguida que se distribuyan a cada uno, y luego con voz
> segura, dice: "aquel cuya varita amanezca mañana más
> grande que las demás es el ladrón". Al día siguiente, fórmase
> de nuevo la tropa, y Quiroga procede a la verificación y
> comparación de las varitas. Un soldado hay, empero, cuya
> vara aparece más corta que las otras. "¡Miserable!, le grita
> Facundo con voz aterrante, ¡tú eres! ... " y en efecto, él era;

> su turbación lo dejaba conocer demasiado. El expediente es
> sencillo : el crédulo gaucho, creyendo que efectivamente
> creciese su varita, le había cortado un pedazo. Pero se necesita
> cierta superioridad y cierto conocimiento de la naturaleza
> humana, para valerse de estos medios. (pp. 51b-52a)

These stories, and hundreds like them, show up the *caudillo* as a
superior being, credited with almost superhuman powers by the
ignorant mob who followed him.

Such, then, is the man who forms the subject of Sarmiento's
acknowledged masterpiece. The rest of the second part is mostly
devoted to an account of his campaigns, a rather dreary narrative
for the ordinary reader, enlivened occasionally by touches of the
kind which we have been shown in the opening chapter of the
second part. One cannot resist the temptation of asking why
Sarmiento devoted so much attention to filling out with a rather
tedious narrative a story whose importance seems to lie mainly in
the character of the protagonist. The explanation must surely be
that he judged it necessary to change a personal attack made
through a kind of *costumbrista* sketch into a full documentary
which had the weight of historical evidence to show the monstrosity of this hated individual and monstrous type, the *gaucho
caudillo*. Although he admits, in the introduction to the work,
that there may have been some mistakes, the representative
character of Quiroga has been his chief aim. All the same he
insists on the general veracity of his account. In a letter written
on the subject and quoted by Paul Verdevoye in one of the most
important and well-documented books produced on our author,
Sarmiento affirms :

> . . . debo declarar que en los acontecimientos notables a que
> me refiero, y que sirven de base a las explicaciones que doy,
> hay una exactitud intachable de que responderán los
> documentos públicos que sobre ellos existen. (*1*, 410)

Clearly Sarmiento took a good deal of trouble in collecting
the material for his documentary study of Facundo Quiroga. In
the introduction to *Facundo* he again says :

He evocado, pues, mis recuerdos, y buscando para completarlos, los detalles que han podido suministrarme hombres que lo conocieron en su infancia, que fueron sus partidarios o sus enemigos, que han visto con sus ojos unos hechos, oído otros, y tenido conocimiento exacto de una época o de una situación particular. Aun espero más datos que los que poseo, que ya son numerosos. (pp. 5b-6a)

The situation is confused by another letter which Verdevoye quotes, dated 22 December 1845, and addressed to General Paz, in which he encloses a copy of *Facundo,* referring to it as "Obra improvisada, llena por necesidad de inexactitudes a designio a veces", and goes on to say that "no tiene otra importancia que la de ser uno de tantos medios para ayudar a destruir un gobierno absurdo; i preparar el camino a otro nuevo" (*1,* 410). Elsewhere again, and this time in a much later statement written on the occasion of the imminent publication of an Italian translation, in 1881, he warned: "No vaya el escalpelo del historiador que busca la verdad gráfica, a herir en las carnes de Facundo, que está vivo; no lo toquéis" (*1,* 411). He anticipates that he will be accused of inaccuracy; but he has the comfort of encouragement from his friends and admirers, one of whom, Vélez Sarsfield, advised him not to change his work because "el Facundo mentira será siempre mejor que el Facundo verdadero" (*1,* 412).

The sources which Sarmiento mentions in the introduction to *Facundo* are his own memories and those of Quiroga's associates; and he mentions that he is awaiting other data. He appears to have obtained these mainly from his reading of the press, and in the appendix to the second edition of the text, which is included in most subsequent editions, he mentions "las gacetas de Buenos Aires", which contain some of Quiroga's statements, including three *proclamas* which are also printed in most of the editions of *Facundo.* The appendix also mentions that some letters of Quiroga have been published; but Sarmiento considers that, like the *proclamas,* "no merecen conservarse sino como curiosidades y monumentos de la época de barbarie" (p. 163b). These were also printed in the Buenos Aires press. Apart from the dismissal of the *proclamas* and letters as unimportant, Sarmiento does draw

some conclusions which are designed to confirm the image of
Quiroga that the author has been concerned to draw throughout
the work :

> Las proclamas que llevan la firma de Juan Facundo
> Quiroga tienen tales caracteres de autenticidad que hemos
> creído útil insertarlas aquí como los únicos documentos
> escritos de aquel caudillo. Campean en ellas la exageración
> y ostentación del propio valor, a la par del no disimulado
> designio de inspirar miedo a los demás. La incorrección del
> lenguaje, la incoherencia de las ideas y el empleo de voces
> que significan otra cosa que lo que se propone expresar en
> ellas o muestran la confusión o el estado embrionario de las
> ideas, revelan en estas proclamas el alma ruda aún, los
> instintos jactanciosos del hombre del pueblo y el candor del
> que, no familiarizado con las letras, ni sospecha siquiera
> que haya incapacidad de su parte para emitir su idea por
> escrito. (p. 163a)

According to Verdevoye's researches Sarmiento did not take
all the trouble he might have done to consult the available sources
for writing Facundo Quiroga's life. In March 1845, the year in
which he wrote the book, one of his correspondents, Antonio
Aberastain, wrote to Sarmiento urging him to take care over the
preparation of a book which would be extremely important, and
telling him of the existence of a collection of Quiroga's letters in
Santiago de Chile. He promised to send him documentary evidence to support a number of observations about Quiroga which
he held to be fundamental. This evidence may well have been the
datos to which Sarmiento referred in his introduction to
Facundo; but Sarmiento does not seem to have had the patience
to await or make full use of this evidence before writing his
book, spurred on as he was by indignation at the arrival in Chile
of the Argentine envoys, led by Baldomero García, who had
come to demand his extradition so that he might be tried for his
alleged crimes against the Argentine state. What is interesting
when one examines the list of characteristics drawn up by
Aberastain is that Sarmiento, in his own account, has shown the
caudillo in a much more favourable light than one would expect,

and has attributed to him a generosity for which there is no
evidence in the summary drawn up by Aberastain. The same
correspondent, in a letter written to Sarmiento four days after
the one referred to, mentions other sources of information which
are sometimes contradictory, and between which he will have to
choose for himself. Whether or not Sarmiento made use of the
documentary material provided by Aberastain and possibly other
correspondents, the evidence itself seems to have disappeared.
Among the oral evidence which Sarmiento used, that provided by
the author's friend Dalmacio Vélez Sarsfield is confirmed, for
what it is worth, by what Sarmiento wrote in his biography of
Vélez Sarsfield himself. Alberdi accused Sarmiento of simply
copying down the stories told him by his friends about Quiroga,
but there seems to be little basis for this accusation, for the
narrative of Quiroga's life and campaigns shows a consistent
line of development, however turgid the story of the latter,
especially, may be.

Quiroga's career as a *caudillo* begins in the province of La
Rioja, in western Argentina, to the north and east of Sarmiento's
native province of San Juan, and bordering on Chile to the south
of the Atacama Desert, inhabited by a patriarchal society of
backward and ignorant peasants. "El *llanista* es el único que
ignora que es el ser más desgraciado, más miserable y bárbaro;
y gracias a esto vive contento y feliz cuando el hambre no le
acosa" (p. 54a). The peace of this remote area was torn by family
feuds. As a result of his part in the attempt to reconcile the
two parties, Facundo Quiroga's father Don Prudencio came to
occupy a position of importance in the political life of the
province. Facundo received his first army command in 1820, and
represented the first incursion of the barbarous society of the
country into civilised life as far as the province of La Rioja was
concerned, although the earlier example of Artigas in what was
later to become Uruguay was a precedent. "Este es un momento
solemne y crítico", says Sarmiento,

en la historia de todos los pueblos pastores de la República
Argentina; hay en todos ellos un día en que, por necesidad de
apoyo exterior, o por temor que ya inspira un hombre audaz,

se elige comandante de campaña. Es este el caballo de los
griegos que los troyanos se apresuraban a introducir en la
ciudad. (p. 54b)

Facundo fought off a force which, failing in their attempts at an
insurrection in the province of San Juan, immediately to the
south of La Rioja, had tried to reassemble in the province where
Facundo was operating. Taking the initiative, Facundo succeeded
in forcing back a much more powerful body, led by two men,
Francisco Aldao and Corro, the first of whom was to provide
Sarmiento with the subject of his first biography, a book which
in some ways can be considered as a trial run for *Facundo*.[56]
Quiroga was entrusted with the task of escorting Aldao back
across the border after the signing of an agreement between him
and the government of La Rioja. Facundo was already dissatis-
fied with the role which was officially assigned to him in La
Rioja, and made a deal with Aldao, who provided him with a
hundred men to enable him to take over power in the northern
province. After a series of skirmishes and intrigues of almost
incredible complication, Quiroga succeeded in establishing himself as ruler of La Rioja. The detail with which Sarmiento tells
this part of the story may well seem excessive to the modern
reader, but it is at least deliberate, for the author regards this
as a crucial landmark in the history and development of modern
Argentina. The year 1823, with the arrival in power of the
caudillo Quiroga in La Rioja, foreshadows the fatal day in April
1835 when Rosas was to take over command of Buenos Aires.
What is very curious is that he holds up his narrative to recall
an action which is to Quiroga's credit. Sarmiento seems to have
been overcome by admiration for the man, and by a sense of
historical occasion, when he writes :

Hay una circunstancia curiosa (1823) que no debo omitir,
porque hace honor a Quiroga; en esta noche negra que
vamos a atravesar, no debe perderse la más leve lucecilla.
Facundo, al entrar triunfante en La Rioja, hizo cesar los

---

56. "El general Fray Félix Aldao", first published in *El Progreso*, 10 Feb., 1845,
    and later under the title *Apuntes biográficos* in *Obras*, VII. The work was
    appended to the second edition of *Facundo* in 1851.

repiques de las campanas, y después de mandar dar el
pésame a la viuda del general muerto, ordenó pomposas
exequias para honrar sus cenizas. Nombró o hizo nombrar
por gobernador a un español vulgar, un Blanco, y con él
precipitó el nuevo orden de cosas que había de realizar el
bello ideal del gobierno que había concebido; porque
Quiroga en su larga carrera, en los diversos pueblos que ha
conquistado, jamás se ha encargado del gobierno organizado,
que abandonaba siempre a otros . . . (p. 57ab)

Sarmiento, going on to develop the idea of how important it is
for a people when it feels itself in the grip of a great man,
clearly regards Quiroga's devolution of authority not only as an
opportunity missed, but as a disaster only to be expected of the
representative of barbarism. Yet curiously enough, in telling
how Quiroga stopped to honour the defeated general, Sarmiento
allows no shade of cynicism to fall over his account, as he might
well have done, and as it was within his purposes to do, for this
action could easily have been interpreted as an attempt to curry
favour with the populace. The account of the administration
which follows is a tale of inefficiency and corruption, of a
primitive denial of all that represents civilisation. Yet the egoism
which Sarmiento sees in Quiroga is "el fondo de casi todos los
grandes caracteres históricos, . . . el muelle real que hace ejecutar
todas las grandes acciones" (p. 59a); it is a political gift and
attribute which the *caudillo* possessed, along with another positive quality, good humour, which Sarmiento spotlights,
providing a number of instances that serve to show only that the
humour is in fact of a rather sick kind. Again there is,
surprisingly, no hint of cynicism in the following account of
what was obviously a very cynical action on the part of Quiroga :

Su buen humor no debe quedar ignorado; necesita
explayarse, extenderlo sobre una gran superficie. Suena la
generala en La Rioja, y los ciudadanos salen a las calles
armados al rumor de alarma. Facundo, que ha hecho tocar a
generala para divertirse, forma a los vecinos en la plaza a
las once de la noche, despide de las filas a la plebe, y deja
sólo a los vecinos padres de familia acomodados, a los
jóvenes que aún conservan visos de cultura.

Háceles marchar y contramarchar toda la noche, hacer
alto, alinearse, marchar de frente, de flanco. Es un cabo
de instrucción que enseña a unos reclutas, y la vara del cabo
anda por la cabeza de los torpes, por el pecho de los que
no se alinean bien : ¿qué quieren? ¡así se enseña! El día
sobreviene, y los semblantes pálidos de los reclutas, su
fatiga y extenuación revelan todo lo que se ha aprendido
en la noche. Al fin da descanso a su tropa, y lleva la
generosidad hasta comprar empanadas, y distribuir a cada
uno la suya, que se apresura a comer, porque es parte ésta de
la diversión. (p. 59ab)

Whether or not Sarmiento had his tongue firmly in his cheek
when he told these anecdotes to illustrate the humour of Quiroga,
it is obvious that he is fond of recounting them, although he
insists that he is giving us only a small selection from the vast
number which recur constantly in all the manuscripts which he
has consulted. He adds : "Sacrifico la relación de ellas a la
vanidad de autor, a la pretensión literaria. Si digo más, los
cuadros me salen recargados, innobles, repulsivos" (p. 61a). In
spite of this lofty claim, one may be forgiven for thinking that
the anecdotes form one of the most attractive parts of the book,
and seem to anticipate some of the more literary short tales which
Ricardo Palma was to include in his ten volumes of *Tradiciones
peruanas*, destined to appear between 1872 and 1910.

With the account of Quiroga's assumption and exercise of
power in La Rioja we have come to the end of what Sarmiento
regards as the first stage in the victory of barbarism over civilisation ultimately epitomised in Rosas, namely the abolition of the
city in favour of the savage self-centred corruption of the
country, whose inhabitants, in the face of the terror which
Quiroga and his men brought to the Llanos, fled to the neighbouring province of San Juan, Sarmiento's own province, not
long destined to enjoy freedom from the tyranny which the
caudillo stood for.

In the meantime, La Rioja has become a war machine which
Quiroga can operate at his will. There was nothing new in this
situation, which had been reached by all the other *caudillos* who
had taken charge of the Argentine provinces or were in the

process of doing so; but Quiroga's fame had spread far beyond
La Rioja, and he was in constant demand from those who
needed help to sustain whatever causes they wished to promote,
causes which were often diametrically opposed to one another.
Ideas were in a state of ferment, not least in the cities, of
which the two outstanding ones were Córdoba, right in the
middle of the Republic and the capital of the province of the
same name; and Buenos Aires. Córdoba, traditional and self-
centred, had actually opposed the 1810 revolution against Spanish
power, and had more or less managed to retain the old courtly
traditions until 1825, shut away from all outside influences and
ideas. Buenos Aires, on the other hand, situated on the banks
of the River Plate and open to the world, had, even before 1810,
fallen under what Sarmiento calls "el ojo especulador de la
Inglaterra" (p. 65b). By 1810 it was teeming with revolutionaries indoctrinated with anti-Spanish and pro-French, European
ideas; ripe for independence. But the fact that Buenos Aires was
so full of revolutionaries, at the same time that it created the
circumstances in which revolution was natural and could easily
triumph, carried its dangers. A modern Venezuelan writer, Juan
Liscano, has suggested that the reason why Argentina has always
tended to revert to dictatorship (he was writing in 1954, during
the first reign of Perón) was that she had never had a great liberal
leader, a Liberator in fact, like Simón Bolívar.[57] It is fair to say
that Sarmiento had already made this point, although naturally
enough he did not draw the same conclusions from it as the
modern writer. The difference between Venezuela and Buenos
Aires — it is significant that the comparison is made with the
capital city and not with the whole state — comes out clearly in
the analysis which Sarmiento makes in the following lines :

> Pero Buenos Aires, en medio de todos estos vaivenes,
> muestra la fuerza revolucionaria de que está dotada. Bolívar
> es todo; Venezuela es la peana de aquella colosal figura.

57. "Sucede que Argentina ha carecido de un gran caudillo, hijo del espíritu y
del pensamiento liberal, que se hiciera caudillo popular y pudiera vencer, en
su propio terreno, a los Facundo, como fue Simón Bolívar y como pudo éste
vencer no solamente a la persona sino también al sentimiento de Boves,
nuestro Facundo". *Ciclo y constantes galleguianos,* Mexico, Ediciones Huma-
nismo, 1954, p 27.

Buenos Aires es una ciudad entera de revolucionarios;
Belgrano, Rondeau, San Martín, Alvear y los cien generales
que mandan sus ejércitos, son sus instrumentos, sus brazos,
no su cabeza ni su cuerpo. En la República Argentina no
puede decirse : "el general tal libertó el país"; sino "la
junta, el directorio, el congreso, el gobierno, de tal o tal
época, mandó al general tal que hiciese tal cosa", etc. El
contacto con los europeos de todas las naciones es mayor aún
desde los principios, que en ninguna parte del continente
hispanoamericano : la *desespañolización* y la *europeificación*
se efectúan en diez años de un modo radical, sólo en Buenos
Aires, se entiende. (p. 66a)

Buenos Aires was under the illusion of another kind of self-
sufficiency, very different from that of Córdoba, believing itself
to be more advanced and European than France itself. The
typical *unitario* from Buenos Aires was a kind of patrician whose
confidence in himself and in the revolutionary future of his
country made him as ostrich-like and as vulnerable as the conservative Cordoban, whose sense of his own importance led even the
cobbler to think of himself as a doctor in cobbling, and who
prided himself in having at least one relative who occupied a
place, however humble, in the ecclesiastical hierarchy. Each
society lacked a well-founded authority, and a real impulse towards federation. It lay waiting for the advance of that barbarism which was embodied in the *caudillos,* and which found its
spearhead in Quiroga, who was to supply the authority for which
the whole country was hungering; but in such a way as to nullify
the civilisation which survived in Córdoba and which was seeking realisation in Buenos Aires. The wandering *gaucho,* of which
type Facundo Quiroga is the perfect example not only by instinct
but by the circumstances of his upbringing, succeeds in trans-
porting his essentially provincial, even parochial, spirit into a
sphere of operations where many of the less ambitious local
gauchos fear to venture :

Efectivamente, Facundo, aunque gaucho, no tiene apego a un
lugar determinado : es riojano, pero se ha educado en San
Juan, ha vivido en Mendoza, ha estado en Buenos Aires.
Conoce la República; sus miradas se extienden sobre un

grande horizonte; dueño de La Rioja, quisiera naturalmente
presentarse revestido del poder en el pueblo en que aprendió
a leer, en las ciudades donde levantó unas tapias, en aquella
otra donde estuvo preso e hizo una acción gloriosa. Si los
sucesos lo atraen fuera de su provincia, no se resistirá a salir
por cortedad ni encogimiento . . . (pp. 70b-71a).

In all this one notes a slight hint of determinism, even of
fatalism. Although he never lacked initiative, it is the circumstances which drive Facundo on to his next step; and they are
the circumstances of his environment as well as of his own temperament and experience. There is a suggestion of inevitability
not only about the career of Quiroga, but also about the course
of events. Buenos Aires was to take the initiative, when its government invited the provinces to assemble in a congress designed
to set up a form of general government. Whether because people
were dazzled by the lure of Buenos Aires, or whether because the
caudillos saw in this a chance of making themselves legitimate
rulers, the idea won universal acceptance. Again there is no hint
of cynicism in Sarmiento's comment that

> Facundo recibió en La Rioja la invitación, y acogió la idea
> con entusiasmo, quizá por aquellas simpatías que los espíritus
> realmente dotados tienen por las cosas esencialmente buenas.
> (p. 72a).

Quiroga was soon to find himself in command of the armed
forces, but exercising a personal rather than a national authority,
and campaigning under a flag of his own invention, bearing,
perhaps significantly and certainly ominously, the skull and cross-
bones. The national colours of Argentina, sky-blue and white,
are replaced by the colour red, henceforward used for the soldiers'
uniform, for the flag of the army, and the emblem of office
(*cucarda*). Sarmiento gives his readers a long excursus on the
significance of the ceremonial use of red at various moments in
world history, all of them associated with sinister events. Before
going on to mention that red was the colour used by Artigas and
to be used later by Rosas, his last remark had been : "El verdugo
en todos los estados europeos vestía de *colorado* hasta el siglo

pasado"; and the common feature he sees in all the manifestations of this colour, past and present, is hinted at in his rhetorical
question : "¿No es el *colorado* el símbolo que expresa violencia,
sangre y barbarie?". He goes on to underline the contrast between the old revolutionary Argentina and the new :

> La revolución de la independencia argentina se simboliza
> en dos tiras celestes y una blanca, cual si dijera : ¡justicia, paz,
> justicia!
> La reacción encabezada por Facundo y aprovechada por
> Rosas, se simboliza en una cinta colorada, que dice : ¡terror,
> sangre, barbarie! (p. 74b)

The symbolic significance which Sarmiento attaches to colour
extends to dress more generally. It will be remembered that when
Sarmiento was in the army he affected the dress of a French
officer of the Napoleonic period; and for civilian wear he saw the
frock-coat as the hall-mark of civilisation itself. The following
passage is significant :

> Aún hay más; cada civilización ha tenido su traje, y cada
> cambio de ideas, cada revolución en las instituciones, un
> cambio en el vestir. Un traje, la civilización romana; otro la
> Edad Media; el frac no principia en Europa sino después del
> renacimiento de las ciencias; la moda no la impone al mundo
> sino la nación civilizada; de frac visten todos los pueblos
> cristianos, y cuando el sultán de Turquía Abdul Madjil quiere
> introducir la civilización en sus estados, depone el turbante,
> el caftán y las bombachas, para vestir frac, pantalón y corbata.
> (p. 75a)

It is significant for Sarmiento that Facundo and Rosas made war
on the *frac,* and that wearing it was enough to invite attack from
their forces, while the red band of the Mazorca of Rosas came to
be essential wear.

The cynicism of Quiroga is well illustrated by Sarmiento when
he tells the story of how, in opposition to the determination of
Buenos Aires to allow freedom of worship, the provinces upheld
the Catholic religion with fanatical zeal. Quiroga, in the province

of San Juan, appeared at the gates of its capital city with a black
flag bearing a red cross and the words : "¡Religión o muerte!"
And this from a man who, as Sarmiento had recorded earlier,
was known never to have attended confession or the Mass, or to
have prayed. Yet his violent action in favour of Catholicism led
to his being described by a famous preacher as "El Enviado de
Dios" (p. 77b).

Sarmiento's own attitude here is an interesting one. Profoundly
influenced in his early days by his uncle José de Oro and other
priests who defended him, the author of *Facundo* always stood
aside from any official religious allegiance or observances; and
his natural tendencies, as well as his reading, pointed towards
free-thinking. Yet at this point in his work Sarmiento seems
quite clearly to identify official religion with barbarism, while
at the same time indicating that there is such a thing as sincere
religion :

> ¿Hubo cuestión religiosa en la República Argentina? Yo lo
> negaría redondamente, si no supiese que cuanto más bárbaro,
> y por tanto más religioso, es un pueblo, tanto más susceptible
> es de preocuparse y fanatizarse. Pero las masas no se movieron···
> espontáneamente, y los que adoptaron aquel lema, Facundo,
> López, Bustos, etc., eran completamente indiferentes. Esto es
> capital. Las guerras religiosas del siglo XV en Europa son
> mantenidas de ambas partes por creyentes sinceros, exaltados,
> fanáticos y decididos hasta el martirio, sin miras políticas, sin
> ambición. Los puritanos leían la Biblia en el momento
> antes del combate, oraban y se preparaban con ayunos y
> penitencias. Sobre todo, el signo en que se conoce el espíritu
> de los partidos, es que realizan sus propósitos cuando llegan
> a triunfar, aun más allá de donde estaban asegurados antes
> de la lucha. Cuando esto no sucede, hay decepción en las pala-
> bras. Después de haber triunfado en la República Argentina
> el partido que se apellida católico, ¿qué ha hecho por la
> religión o los intereses del sacerdocio? (p. 78a)

There seems little point in following in detail the chaotic course
of Quiroga's career as a *caudillo,* with its mixture of violence,
cynicism, opportunism and inconstancy, enlivened by anecdotes
which often show a side of his character that his biographer seems

to have found attractive almost in spite of himself. One episode will illustrate that "el alma de Facundo no estaba del todo cerrada a las nobles inspiraciones" (p. 92b); another that, as Sarmiento has observed that modern dramatists have found to their advantage, "aun en los caracteres históricos más negros, hay siempre una chispa de virtud que alumbra por momentos y se oculta" (p. 93a).

Quiroga's gifts as a *caudillo* cannot fail to recall in many ways those of the Peninsular *guerrilleros* who sprang into public life during the wars against Napoleon's forces after the invasion of Spain in 1808, and who come to life so vividly in Pérez Galdós's *Juan Martín el Empecinado,* surviving into civilian life as thugs like Caballuco in the same novelist's *Doña Perfecta.* Quiroga, all through his successful career as a *caudillo,* never loses the characteristics of the *gaucho,* and in particular of the *gaucho malo,* the outlaw. He illustrates Sarmiento's point that "si levantáis un poco las solapas del frac con que el argentino se disfraza, hallaréis siempre el gaucho más o menos civilizado, pero siempre el gaucho" (p. 99a). This is the theme which constantly recurs, and again there is a suggestion of determinism as the biographer insists that Facundo is essentially neither cruel nor bloodthirsty, but simply a barbarian, governed by instincts of violence which, indulged and exalted into a system and a way of life, were then coldly and deliberately exploited by Rosas.

Against the barbarous individualism of the *caudillos* the upholder of the idea of a real federation in Argentina, and the successor to General San Martín, the Liberator of the Republic, stood José María Paz to whom Sarmiento directed a stirring appeal at the end of *Facundo* (p. 161ab).[58] Paz, in order to avoid bloodshed, proposed a settlement with Quiroga, who at the end of 1830 was advancing on Córdoba with a combined army drawn from the provinces of La Rioja, San Juan, Mendoza and San Luis. Facundo refused these overtures, but was outwitted by Paz,

58. It was in a letter to Paz dated 22 December 1845 that Sarmiento wrote of *Facundo,* of which he was sending a copy to the general, as "Obra improvisada, llena por necesidad de inexactitudes a designio a veces, no tiene otra importancia que la de ser uno de tantos medios para ayudar a destruir un gobierno absurdo; preparar el camino a otro nuevo" (quoted *I,* 410).

who in the battle showed a skill which Sarmiento considers to have been worthy of comparison with that of Napoleon, and who inflicted a resounding defeat upon the *caudillo* and his forces. Now the provinces of Córdoba, Mendoza, San Juan, San Luis, La Rioja, Catamarca, Tucumán, Salta and Jujuy were liberated from the forces of barbarism, and General Paz was able to summon an assembly with a view to setting up an orderly constitutional government. His efforts were thwarted, however, by the developments which were taking place in Buenos Aires, where Rosas was achieving the ascendancy. The curious situation had come about whereby the provinces were overwhelmingly in favour of setting up a Union with Buenos Aires as capital; whereas in Buenos Aires the desire was to shake off any kind of responsibility which would be associated with European civilisation and civil order. The defeat of the *caudillos* under Quiroga led to their loss of morale, and Facundo had to rely more and more on terrorism to maintain his sway; while in Buenos Aires the civil authority was more and more undermined by the power of the *gauchos* assembled under Rosas, until they finally gained the upper hand, through a curious reversal of the traditional roles whereby Lavalle, the leader of the Buenos Aires cavalry, adopted guerrilla tactics, only to find that Rosas abandoned his horses and relied on infantry attacks. In this strange situation, the *gauchos* won the day, and the cause of Argentine civilisation suffered almost irrevocable harm in the capital. In the meantime, surprisingly, Paz's régime in Córdoba brought to that city the fruits of modern civilisation in a way which had never been known before, and Facundo, by an ironic twist, was forced to take refuge in Buenos Aires, where he threw in his lot with Rosas and López, the successor to Artigas, eventually to lead an attack on the provinces, and on Córdoba, now the centre of civilisation. Quiroga first advanced upon the province of San Luis, to the south-west of Córdoba, with a force of three hundred men, and then continued westwards to Mendoza where, by using the traditional guerrilla tactics of the *gauchos,* he managed to defeat a much greater cavalry force. To this reliance on cavalry Sarmiento attributes a hundred battles lost to the Argentine Republic "porque el espíritu de la Pampa está allí en todos los corazones" (p. 99a).

As a result of this victory achieved in the battle of Chacón, Quiroga was in a position to outflank the forces of Córdoba province, which were at that time about to set out themselves to make an attack upon Buenos Aires. The audacity of Quiroga's strategy struck terror into the neighbouring provinces, and San Juan, Cuyo and La Rioja fell into his hands almost without effort. The precarious foothold of civilisation found itself undermined; and the considerable achievements of the province of Mendoza were trampled by the brutish forces of Facundo and his barbarians. The atrocities committed by the *gauchos* are related by Sarmiento with all the force of his considerable rhetoric, and one cannot help recalling the tirades of the Dominican Bartolomé de las Casas, "the Apostle of the Indies", as he fulminated against the savagery and inhuman behaviour of the Spaniards in their American colonies in the sixteenth century.[59]

From Mendoza Quiroga's forces made their way to San Juan and thence to Tucumán, where the forces of Córdoba province had retreated after the loss of their general, Villafañe. Sarmiento describes with feeling the scenes of horror of the ruthless *caudillo* in his native province of San Juan, culminating in the barbarous cruelty to which he was party on the day on which the expedition set out for Tucumán. In a curious kind of way, Sarmiento seems to be making an attempt to excuse Quiroga's behaviour, while at the same time underlining the monstrosity of it. He writes :

> Y sin embargo de todo esto, Facundo no es cruel, no es sanguinario : es el bárbaro, no más, que no sabe contener sus pasiones, y que, una vez irritadas, no conocen freno ni medida; es el terrorista que a la entrada de una ciudad fusila a uno y azota a otro; pero con economía, muchas veces con discernimiento; el fusilado es un ciego, un paralítico, o un sacristán; cuando más, el infeliz azotado es un ciudadano ilustre, un joven de las primeras familias. Sus brutalidades con las señoras vienen de que no tiene conciencia de las delicadas atenciones que la debilidad merece; las humillaciones afrentosas impuestas a los ciudadanos provienen de que es campesino grosero y gusta por ello de maltratar y herir en

59. See especially the *Brevísima relación de la destrucción de las Indias*, first published in 1552.

el amor propio y el decoro a aquellos que sabe que lo
desprecian. No es otro el motivo que hace del terror un
sistema de gobierno . . . (p. 105b)

There is a strange kind of detachment and yet of fascination, like
that which one might have while watching a cat kill a bird, at the
same time horrified yet recognising that the cat is doing what
comes naturally.

This natural barbarity was taken up and deliberately exploited
by Rosas, who made of terror his chosen instrument. The
difference between the two leaders is strikingly summed up in
the following brief paragraph, which concludes the seventh
chapter of this second part of *Facundo* :

> Pero Facundo es cruel sólo cuando la sangre se le ha
> venido a la cabeza y a los ojos, y ve todo colorado. Sus
> cálculos fríos se limitan a fusilar a un hombre, azotar a un
> ciudadano; Rosas no se enfurece nunca : calcula en la
> quietud de su gabinete, y desde allí salen las órdenes a sus
> sicarios. (p. 106b)

Although Rosas from now on emerges more and more clearly
from the background, the story continues to be centred round
Facundo, to whom we return as he is on the point of setting out
from San Juan to Tucumán, leaving a sense of profound relief
among the federals and the wives and mothers of the unitarians.
Defending Tucumán was General La Madrid, one of whose
subordinates was General López, described as a kind of *caudillo*
of Tucumán and opposed to his superior. In other words, the
defence of the province was divided, while the attacking forces
under Quiroga were united by the terror which he had succeeded
in inspiring in them. This terror spread to the city of Tucumán,
whose population had fled at the appearance of the Tiger of
the Plains, leaving it prey to the terror which had already put
back the clock in the province of Mendoza : a terror which, as
always instinctive in Facundo, became a calculated weapon of
annihilation in the hands of Rosas, whose use of terrifying words
was even more effective than the horrific deeds of his subordinates – if subordinate could ever be used of such a man as

Quiroga. The fascination which Sarmiento could not help feeling and expressing for the local *caudillo*, whether or not a manifestation of that romantic titanism to which students of Sarmiento have referred,[60] was inevitably extended to Rosas, of whom it is difficult to think as the arch-villain of Argentine nineteenth-century history, in the way that undoubtedly Sarmiento did think of him formally and deliberately. He writes:

> ¡Rosas! ¡Rosas! ¡me posterno y humillo ante su poderosa inteligencia! ¡Sois grande como el Plata; como los Andes! ¡Sólo tú has comprendido cuan despreciable es la especie humana, sus libertades, su ciencia y su orgullo! . . . (p. 112b)

But the sting is in the tail:

> ¡Pisoteadla! ¡que todos los gobiernos del mundo civilizado te atacarán a medida que seas más insolente! ¡Pisoteadla! ¡que no te faltarán perros fieles que, recogiendo el mendrugo que les tiras, vayan a derramar su sangre en los campos de batalla, o a ostentar en el pecho vuestra marca colorada por todas las capitales americanas! ¡Pisoteadla! ¡oh! sí, ¡Pisoteadla! . . . (p. 112b)

Thanks to Rosas, the twenty years from 1825 to 1845 have been lost, and more still will be wasted until God wills to crush the monster of the *pampa*; but "no hay males que sean eternos" (p. 114a), Sarmiento concludes, and on this note of resigned hopefulness he ends his eighth chapter of the second part of *Facundo*.

At this juncture Quiroga, having conquered the provinces from Salta in the north to San Luis in the south, has disbanded his army, leaving the territory in uneasy peace under the shadow of Quiroga's baneful influence. Federalism is dead, and Quiroga is pressing for election as president of the Republic the ex-governor of San Luis, Dr. José Santos Ortiz, his friend and secretary, urging his claims in the following disingenuous terms: "No es gaucho como yo: es doctor y hombre de bien, dice: sobre todo, el hombre que sabe hacer justicia a sus enemigos merece

60. Cf. above, p. 27.

toda confianza" (p. 115b). While nominally renouncing his powers like some sinister John the Baptist, he was effectively keeping control of affairs in his own hands. But the shadow of Rosas was already looming not only over the area of the River Plate, but also over the figure of his former ally and now his rival. Once more Buenos Aires was about to cast its mantle over the provinces of the interior. Sarmiento shows how back in 1822 the Republic was divided into the two great areas associated with the Andes and the River Plate, the former dominated by Quiroga and the latter by the Liga Litoral, which more and more as time went on was to mean effectively by Rosas. The crisis came when Quiroga, unannounced, and perhaps in response to some deep yearning for civilisation, Sarmiento suggests, came with his entourage to Buenos Aires, where he found himself the centre of the most influential men in the capital, and enjoying all the signs of power and prestige. The old *caudillo* sends his sons to the best schools and insists that they wear European dress and adopt civil careers, while he succumbs more and more to the softening influences of civilisation . . .

Y mientras tanto que se abandona así a una peligrosa indolencia, ve cada día acercarse la boa que ha de sofocarlo en sus redobladas lanzas (read 'lazadas') . . . (p. 120a)

Quiroga was called upon to suppress unrest in the north of the Republic, and set off, after some show of reluctance, in December 1835. Hampered by a shortage of horses, and threatened with assassination in Córdoba, he managed to settle the differences between the contending governors, and returned to Córdoba in spite of many attempts to dissuade him. Now acting almost as if he had a date with destiny, which he had already hinted at as he left Buenos Aires for his last campaign, he yet hurls defiance at those who warn him of the dangers which await him. To a loyal young supporter, Sandivaras, he turns aside the offer of a way of escape with the words: "No ha nacido todavía . . . el hombre que ha de matar a Facundo Quiroga. A un grito mío, esa partida mañana se pondrá a mis órdenes y me servirá de escolta hasta Córdoba. Vaya usted, amigo, sin cuidado" (p. 123b).

In spite of the efforts of his terrified secretary, Dr. Ortiz, who knows all the details of the planned assassination, Facundo rushes headlong into the face of danger, a danger which found its embodiment in a *gaucho malo* not unlike Quiroga himself, one who, Sarmiento tells us, could have been a worthy rival of Facundo, but who ended up a mere hired assassin, acting under orders from the Reinafé brothers, themselves the agents of Rosas. The government of Buenos Aires, perhaps ironically in the circumstances, took it upon itself to execute the assassins.

Sarmiento's account of the last days of Quiroga is a masterpiece of suspense until the moment of his death, when the story is told briefly and graphically, ending with a terse statement which is worth quoting for its pointed economy, reminding us of the art which Menéndez Pidal attributed to the composers of the old Spanish ballads – *saber callar a tiempo* :

El gobierno de Buenos Aires dio un aparato solemne a la ejecución de los asesinos de Juan Facundo Quiroga. La galera ensangrentada [in which Quiroga and his secretary had been travelling when the attack on them took place] y acribillada a balazos estuvo largo tiempo expuesta a examen del pueblo; y el retrato de Quiroga, como la vista del patíbulo y de los ajusticiados, fueron litografiados y distribuidos por millares como también extractos del proceso, que se dio a luz en un volumen en folio. La historia imparcial espera todavía datos y revelaciones para señalar con su dedo al instigador de los asesinos. (p. 125b)

9. Tercera parte

It will be remembered that this third part was omitted from the second edition of *Facundo* (1851);[61] and the effect of the closing paragraph of the Segunda Parte must have been a very powerful one. Readers would know perfectly well where Sarmiento stood in relation to Rosas and his régime, and would know exactly in which direction the writer's finger was pointing in the last sentence. What the Tercera Parte does is to make explicit Sarmiento's hatred for the régime at whose hands he had suffered so much. But like the endings to the ballad of the Conde Arnaldos, which clear up the mystery of the older version with its haunting ending, "Yo no digo esta canción,/sino a quien conmigo va", this third part adds a rather long coda. It reminds one of those concluding chapters which nineteenth-century novelists like Valera included to let us know what happened to the characters who were not in the picture at the end of the main narrative, because in the final instance they were secondary, if not exactly minor, characters. This is the role in which Sarmiento has cast Rosas, and he insists that, as he had said in his introduction,

> . . . para mi entender, Facundo Quiroga es el núcleo de la guerra civil de la República Argentina, y la expresión más franca y candorosa de una de las fuerzas que han luchado con diversos nombres durante treinta años. La muerte de Quiroga no es un hecho aislado sin consecuencias; antecedentes sociales que he desenvuelto antes, la hacían casi inevitable; era un desenlace político, como el que podría haber dado una guerra. (p. 129a)

Facundo's death took place on 18 February 1835, and the news of it reached Buenos Aires by the 24th. It did not take Rosas long to prepare the way for his assumption of power,

61. Cf. above, The Structure of *Facundo*.

which was effected on 5 April, when the Junta de Representantes elected him governor for five years. For once we can hardly exonerate Sarmiento from writing with his tongue in his cheek when he follows the name of the newly-elected governor with the titles "Héroe del Desierto, Ilustre Restaurador de las Leyes, Depositario de la Suma del Poder Público" (p. 130a). The last sobriquet did in fact give rise to some doubts and questions, and Sarmiento asks how, in a province of 400,000 inhabitants, it came about that there were only three votes recorded against the Rosas government, according to the *Gaceta*:

> . . . ¿Sería acaso que los disidentes no votaron? ¡Nada de eso! No se tiene aún noticia de ciudadano alguno que no fuese a votar; los enfermos se levantaron de la cama para ir a dar su asentimiento, temerosos de que sus nombres fuesen inscritos en algún negro registro, porque así se había insinuado. (p. 130a)

The explanation Sarmiento gives is quite simply that the terror has arrived, and that this vote, unique in the annals of civilised peoples, indicates a total weariness and loss of spirit on the part of a nation worn down by ceaseless, unremitting struggle, and longing, as so many have done in the course of history, for peace at any price. Once established, the mixture of inertia and terror became almost irresistible, and the solution arrived at irreversible.

The deep hatred and contempt which Sarmiento has kept bottled up for so long is no more capable of being restrained, and the picture of the new governor as he takes up office on 13 April 1835 is one that shows the dangerous subtlety of his character, which has been hinted at before, in contrast to the hasty impulsiveness of Quiroga. Those who expected to see a clumsy *gaucho*, embarrassed by the solemnity of the occasion, found instead one who had chosen every detail of gesture and dress to drive home the novelty of the new régime, its emphasis on personal control and on terror:

> De la Sala de Representantes, adonde ha ido a recibir el bastón, se retira en un coche *colorado*, mandado pintar exprofeso para el acto, al que están atados cordones de seda

colorada, y a los que se uncen aquellos hombres que desde 1833 han tenido la ciudad en continua alarma por sus atentados y su impunidad; llámase la *Sociedad Popular,* y lleva *puñal* a la cintura, chaleco *colorado,* y una cinta *colorada,* en la que se lee: *Mueran los unitarios.* En la puerta de su casa le hacen guardia de honor estos mismos hombres; después acuden los ciudadanos, después los generales, porque es necesario hacer aquella manifestación de adhesión sin límites a la persona del Restaurador. (p. 132a)

Although the hatred which Sarmiento felt for Rosas seems to have gone deeper than the feelings he entertained for Facundo Quiroga, one cannot altogether get away from the hint of admiration for the monster which shows through from time to time. In telling of the dictator's physical energy, for instance, Sarmiento classes him with Napoleon and Byron; and he recalls how Rosas was prepared to suffer punishment for his own breach of the laws for which he had been responsible :

. . . En cuanto al cuchillo, ninguno de sus peones lo cargó jamás, no obstante que la mayor parte de ellos eran asesinos perseguidos por la justicia. Una vez él, por olvido, se ha puesto el puñal a la cintura, y el mayordomo se lo hace notar; Rosas se baja los calzones y manda que se le den los doscientos azotes, que es la pena impuesta en su estancia al que lleva cuchillo. (p. 135b)

What has been described as Sarmiento's titanism, or alternatively what might be his inability to resist a good story, finally makes a human being of the redoubtable Rosas; and although Sarmiento may have damaged his purpose by yielding to these tendencies, there is no doubt that the book as such is all the better for it.

Despite these lighter touches, the indictment of Rosas and his régime engenders a good deal of anger and impatience in the writer of *Facundo.* In one way and another every deed of the dictator contributed to the hardening of the arteries, to the exclusiveness and backwardness of the Argentine Republic. One clash which demonstrated very well for Sarmiento the bigotry of his old enemy was the attitude to the French, who had sided with the old unitarians, and whose nationals found themselves badly treated by the new régime, and decided to blockade the city of Buenos Aires, to the intense delight of Rosas, who saw the opportunity to rally the sentiments and forces of *americanismo*. This was the occasion for the outbreak of all the forces of barbarism and anti-Europeanism, which for Sarmiento were essentially the same thing.

After two years the French abandoned their blockade, apparently a complete failure, with the ships rotting in the waters of the River Plate; but the disastrous results, as Sarmiento sees them, of the upsurge of national sentiment which the blockade brought forth, were followed by yet one more step down into the abyss of barbarism, about which he writes in the second and concluding chapter of this short third part of *Facundo*. The more civilised elements of Buenos Aires society had taken refuge on the Banda Oriental of the river, in Montevideo, later to be the capital city of the new Republic of Uruguay. There they were joined by the disaffected followers of Rosas, and eventually by the younger generation who had grown up under the terror but who had kept in touch with European civilisation through their reading of predominantly French works, and who formed a Salón Literario, the breeding-ground, Sarmiento asserts, of most of the distinguished men of letters, and the creators of an Acta, a liberal document whose tenets brought them into danger from the régime. It was these young people, among whom Sarmiento counts himself, who allied themselves with the French forces which blockaded Buenos Aires for the sake of saving European values, and civilisation, from the attacks of destructive barbarism, of what Sarmiento now repeatedly calls *americanismo*.

This *americanismo,* upheld by Rosas through terror and murder, made of Buenos Aires, according to Sarmiento's account, a *teatro sangriento,* from which citizens fled in their multitudes, mixing with the *gauchos* of the country areas in a kind of fellowship of misfortune. The country, which had been in Rosas's hands, abandoned him, and he came more and more to depend on a band of thugs who were attached to him by personal allegiance, which became in the course of time less firm through mutual jealousies and conspiracies, paralysing and reducing to impotence any kind of progress.

It was in the end the French government, official France, which ended the blockade and came to terms with Rosas, showing what Sarmiento considers to be an insensitivity to the cause of advancement and civilisation, in which official England, whose commercial interests were also involved, shared to an astonishing degree. England, by her indifference, has in fact been secretly aiding the forces of barbarism, and has been denying her own real interests. In a series of rhetorical questions Sarmiento taunts England with her shortsightedness :

. . . ¿Quiere la Inglaterra consumidores, cualquiera que el gobierno de un país sea? Pero ¿qué han de consumir seiscientos mil gauchos pobres, sin industrias como sin necesidades, bajo un gobierno que, extinguiendo las costumbres y gustos europeos, disminuye necesariamente el consumo de productos europeos? ¿Habremos de creer que la Inglaterra desconoce hasta este punto sus intereses en América? ¿Ha querido poner su mano poderosa para que no se levante en el Sur de la América un Estado como el que ella engendró en el Norte? (p. 151a)

Now, for virtually the first time in the whole book, Sarmiento sounds a note of optimism about the future of the Argentine Republic, finding curiously, even paradoxically in view of what he has previously said about the *pampa,* the strength of the country in that same *pampa,* "en las producciones tropicales del Norte y en el gran sistema de ríos navegables cuya aorta es el Plata. Por otra parte", he continues, surprising us again by aligning himself with the Spaniards for whom he has previously professed such hatred, "los españoles no somos ni navegantes ni industriosos, y la Europa nos proveerá por largos siglos de sus artefactos en cambio de nuestras materias primas, y ella y nosotros ganaremos en el cambio; la Europa nos pondrá el remo en la mano y nos remolcará río arriba hasta que hayamos adquirido el gusto de la navegación" (p. 151ab).

Sarmiento adduces another and a rather curious reason for his optimism, namely that the personal power of Rosas has stifled the influence of the other *caudillos,* who might have threatened a constitutional government, so that when such a government is established, the opposition from local leaders will already have been overcome, and a united republic will be a possibility. Sarmiento already foresees the day when the terror of Rosas will be reduced to that of a sort of bogey-man, a national curiosity which will attract the notice of visitors from abroad as a kind of tourist attraction.

In the meantime the Rosas régime is a present reality, and the struggle between civilisation and barbarism goes on, proof of this being found in the fact that not a single writer or poet has been found on the side of the tyrant. "¿Por qué", Sarmiento asks pointedly, "la poesía ha abandonado a Rosas?" (p. 155b). The indifference of Rosas towards civilisation shows in the total lack of any attempt at a real administration. Rosas has not fostered commerce or industry. These tasks, together with the fixing of frontiers and the security of national territory, as well as a policy of foreign immigration, await the new government. Under this new government will flourish improved navigation and other forms of communication, along with colleges and schools and a free press and publishing industry. Men will enjoy freedom to pursue enlightenment, protected by justice, and be at liberty to worship and to hold convictions. They will form once more part of the commonwealth of nations, bound by peaceful and civilised ties to Europe as well as to their neighbours in America.

If the note which Sarmiento sounds at the end of his book is not exactly apocalyptic, the prophecies which he makes are almost unbelievably optimistic when one considers the situation at the time he was writing, when the Rosas régime had another seven years of terror still to run. "Puede ser", he writes,

que tantos bienes no se obtengan de pronto, y que después de una subversión tan radical como la que ha obrado Rosas, cueste todavía un año o más de oscilaciones hacer entrar a la sociedad en sus verdaderos quicios. Pero con la caída de ese monstruo, entraremos, por lo menos, en el camino que conduce a porvenir tan bello, en lugar de que bajo su funesta impulsión nos alejamos más cada día, y vamos a pasos agigantados retrocediendo a la barbarie, a la desmoralización y a la pobreza . . . (p. 157b)

Argentina, "Unitaria, federal, mixta, . . . ha de salir de los hechos consumados" (p. 158a), following the example of her neighbour Peru. The future president of the Republic reasserts his faith in humanity, even in the humanity spoiled and distorted by the corruption of the Rosas régime. The country will enter into its rich natural heritage and the revolution, begun so long ago, will at last be consummated, in a unity which the dictator himself will have helped to bring about. The book ends with a kind of *quod erat demonstrandum* :

> Creo haber demostrado que la revolución de la República Argentina está ya terminada y que sólo la existencia del execrable tirano que ella engendró estorba que hoy mismo entre en una carrera no interrumpida de progreso que pudieran envidiarle bien pronto algunos pueblos americanos. La lucha de las campañas con las ciudades, se ha acabado; el odio a Rosas ha reunido a estos elementos; los antiguos federales y los viejos unitarios, como la nueva generación, han sido perseguidos por él y se han unido. (p. 160ab; cf. *12*, 279)

It is now up to the people, and especially to General Paz, to whom Sarmiento makes a final appeal, to save the Republic from the monster which has so long held it in thrall.

10. Conclusion

Despite its later fame, at least as a work of literature, the immediate impact of *Facundo* was not a world-shattering one. The sales of the first edition of 1845 were poor, and it must have been with mixed feelings that Sarmiento heard Rosas's reaction, reported by Bunkley : "This is the best thing that has been written against me; that is the way to attack someone, sir; you will see that no one will defend me so ably" (*6*, 208). It was not until 1846, when a favourable review of *Facundo* appeared in the *Revue des Deux Mondes* of 15 November, that the work began to acquire fame, although it seems that its appeal was primarily the result of its picturesque portrayal of a part of the world which hitherto had been largely unknown (cf. *1*, 429-30). After this the work enjoyed considerable success both at home and abroad, and appears to have been used as a weapon by the underground opposition, if one can envisage such a phenomenon, under the reign of Rosas. Apart from the four editions in Spanish published during Sarmiento's lifetime, the work was translated either wholly or in part into French several times and into Italian once before his death in 1888; and mention has already been made of Mrs. Mann's English translation published in New York in 1868. German and Portuguese translators have appeared during the present century (*1*, 544-5), and the number of studies of this work runs into hundreds. Despite its faults, it must remain a seminal work for all students of Argentine history and sociology; but its primary appeal continues to be that of a work of literature, uneven and sometimes confusing, but rarely dull, rising to the height of poetry on occasion, and always full of energy, keen perception and imagination.

Select Bibliography

1. For a detailed bibliography of Sarmiento's writings and of studies of him and his works, reference should be made to Paul Verdevoye's *Domingo Faustino Sarmiento éducateur et publiciste (entre 1839 et 1852)*, Paris, 1963.

BIOGRAPHY

2. Lugones, Leopoldo, *Historia de Sarmiento*, Buenos Aires, 1931. (A eulogy of the author, commissioned by the Argentine Government.)

3. Gálvez, Manuel, *Vida de Sarmiento. El hombre de autoridad*, 3rd edition, Buenos Aires, Tor, n.d. (An unfavourable view of Sarmiento.)

4. Rojas, Ricardo, *El profeta de la pampa. Vida de Sarmiento*, Buenos Aires, Losada, 1945. (The most massive biography of Sarmiento, with many quotations and anecdotes, but no index or bibliography.)

5. Palcos, Alberto, *Sarmiento: la vida – la obra – las ideas – el genio*, 4th edition, Buenos Aires, 1962. (The best general work on the author in Spanish.)

6. Bunkley, Allison W., *The Life of Sarmiento*, Princeton University Press, 1952. (The best general work on the author in English.)

HISTORICAL BACKGROUND

7. Chapman, Charles E., *Republican Hispanic America: A History*, New York, Macmillan, 1938. (Very useful on the *gaucho* and on caudillism.)

8. Herring, Hubert, *A History of Latin America*, 3rd edition, London, Jonathan Cape, 1961. (Probably the best general history of Latin America.)

CRITICAL STUDIES

9. Unamuno, Miguel de, "Algunas consideraciones sobre la literatura hispano-americana", in *Ensayos*, VII, Madrid, 1918, 99-156. (Emphasises Sarmiento's "Spanish-ness".)

10. Palcos, Alberto, *El Facundo. Rasgos de Sarmiento*, Buenos Aires, 2nd edition, 1945. (Useful on the different early editions of *Facundo*, and on the problem of its classification.)

11. Castro, Américo, "En torno al *Facundo* de Sarmiento", in *Sur*, VIII, August 1938, 26-34. (Develops the designation of *Facundo* as a history book in the romantic manner.)

12. Barrenechea, Ana María, "Notas al estilo de Sarmiento", in *Revista iberoamericana*, 21, 1956, 275-94. (Discusses the mixture of spontaneity and careful planning in *Facundo*.)

13. id., "Las ideas de Sarmiento antes de la publicación del *Facundo*", in *Filología*, V, 1959, 193-210. (Shows how, before *Facundo*, Sarmiento tended to explain everything in terms of the Spanish heritage.)

14. Alberdi, Juan Bautista, *La barbarie histórica de Sarmiento*, Buenos Aires, 1964. (The work was written in 1862, and represents a hostile view of Sarmiento and his work.)

15. Salomon, Noël, "A propos des éléments 'costumbristas' dans le *Facundo* de D. F. Sarmiento", in *Bulletin Hispanique*, LXX, 1968, 342-412. (Discusses Sarmiento's debt to Larra and Spanish *costumbrismo*.)